# SNOD THIS
# for a
# LAUGH

# SNOD
# THIS
## for a
# LAUGH

Sport Media

# SNOD THIS for a LAUGH

Sport Media

Copyright: Ian Snodin
Written by: Alan Jewell
Editorial & Proofing: James Cleary
Statistics: Gavin Buckland

Business Development Director: Mark Dickinson. Executive Editor: Ken Rogers.
Senior Editor: Steve Hanrahan. Editor: Paul Dove. Senior Art Editor: Rick Cooke.
Sales and Marketing Manager: Elizabeth Morgan.
Sales and Marketing Assistant: Karen Cadman.
Sport Media Marketing Executive: Claire Brown.

Cover design: Lee Ashun.

ISBN: 9781906802578

Photographs:
Trinity Mirror, Mirrorpix, PA Pics, Ian Snodin collection

Printed by CPI Mackay

# IN PROFILE

## Ian Snodin

**Full name:** Ian Snodin
**Birthplace:** Thryberg, Rotherham
**Height:** 5'10"
**Weight:** 9st. 7lbs
**Home:** Thryberge
**Previous Club:** None
**Trade before turning professional:** None
**Car:** None
**Club nickname:** Snod
**Worst ever injury:** Torn knee ligaments
**Favourite British teams:** Chelsea
**Favourite Stadium where played:** Ibrox (Glasgow Rangers)
**Best goal scored:** My first league goal against Aldershot two years ago
**Most difficult opponent:** There are a few
**Personal magic moment in football:** Being made captain and playing for England Youth
**Biggest dissapointment:** Not beating Dennis Peacock at gates
**Favourite other sports:** Golf, cricket, badminton
**Miscellaneous likes:** Winning, listening to music
**Miscellaneous dislikes:** Losing and not playing well
**Favourite TV programme:** Fawlty Towers, Benny Hill
**Favourite Muscian/bands:** George Benson, The Jam
**Favourite Food:** Steak, fish and chips
**Favourite drink:** Milk
**Favourite actor:** Charles Bronson
**Favourite actress:** Jane Fonda
**Biggest influence:** Dad and Coaching Staff at Belle Vue
**Susperstitions:** None
**Personal ambition:** To be happy and healthy
**Professional ambition:** To play in the First Division
**Career after playing:** To be Alan Warboys' bank manager

# SNOD THIS FOR A LAUGH

## SEEING THE FUNNY SIDE

I DO a lot of after-dinner speaking engagements and I enjoy giving people an insight into what happened during my professional career. People want to hear genuine stories.

I was half-decent as a footballer and half-decent as a lad. I knew when to be serious but I could have a laugh as well.

Nobody hated losing more than me. My children will tell you that – whether we're playing golf or tennis, I am always desperate to win.

I don't think I'm more important than any of my mates, just because I played for Everton and was called up to a couple of England squads. I'm absolutely not. I'm simply a lucky lad who played football and enjoyed life to the full.

I've read some footballers' books and they tend to be same old, same old, same old. Hopefully my effort will offer an insight into the lads I played alongside and against, giving an overall picture of what footballers got up to during my era.

It wasn't a case of playing a match on a Saturday and retreating to your house; there was more to it than that.

We were paid nicely but we were just genuine, normal people. Anybody who knows me understands I'm not big-time at all. I wasn't allowed to become like that because my dad and Billy Bremner would have kicked my arse everywhere if I had.

I hope you enjoy this book and see the funny side of my career, and the people who shared it with me.

**Ian Snodin**

## ODDS AND SNODS

WRITING this book with Ian Snodin has been an educational experience.

His hilarious tales bring into sharp focus just how much football has changed over the last 20 years.

The various stories, scrapes and escapades are of their time. Ian says himself that he is glad he played when he did. His man-of-the-people personality isn't suited to the sport in the 21st century, which far too often takes itself far too seriously.

That's not an accusation you could level at Mr Snodin.

I have become used to being addressed as "pal", his favourite term of endearment. A text message from him will contain at least one such reference, frequently more.

Initial progress towards compiling this publication wasn't so much slow as glacial. Ian is a busy man who spends a significant portion of his life on the M62, commuting between his two bases: Doncaster and Liverpool. He was difficult to pin down and scheduled arrangements didn't always lead to a meeting.

On one occasion I was watching the clock in my office as the appointed hour for one of our conversations came and went. Sixty minutes ticked by with no word. Then a colleague called to reveal he had just seen Ian in the William Hill betting shop a few hundred yards away.

Well, it was the first day of the Aintree Grand National meeting.

On the afternoon we took the cover photograph for this book, Ian texted me to say he would be half-an-hour late. Before his arrival, I nipped into the same William Hill's to pick up a few betting slips for use as potential props. You can probably guess who I found staring at the television screen, watching the 2.20 at York.

Happily, once we were into our stride, the book quickly took shape, the result of a series of meetings at my office,

Thomas Rigby's courtyard in Liverpool, the Stag and Rainbow in West Derby, Goodison Park, Relish Bar and Grill in Doncaster and a couple of motorway service stations.

And, despite what you'll read in the following pages, he hasn't touched a drop of alcohol during the whole process.

**Alan Jewell, Co-author**

PLAYERS:

| | | | |
|---|---|---|---|
| 1 | PETER SHILTON | – | DERBY COUNTY |
| 2 | DAVID SEAMAN | – | QUEENS PARK RANGERS |
| 3 | GARY STEVENS | – | GLASGOW RANGERS |
| 4 | STUART PEARCE | – | NOTTINGHAM FOREST |
| 5 | IAN SNODIN | – | EVERTON |
| 6 | TONY DORIGO | – | CHELSEA |
| 7 | TERRY BUTCHER | – | GLASGOW RANGERS |
| 8 | DES WALKER | – | NOTTINGHAM FOREST |
| 9 | TONY ADAMS | – | ARSENAL |
| 10 | PAUL PARKER | – | QUEENS PARK RANGERS |
| 11 | NEIL WEBB | – | NOTTINGHAM FOREST |
| 12 | BRYAN ROBSON | – | MANCHESTER UNITED |
| 13 | PAUL DAVIS | – | ARSENAL |
| 14 | STEVE HODGE | – | NOTTINGHAM FOREST |
| 15 | PAUL GASCOIGNE | – | TOTTENHAM HOTSPUR |
| 16 | DAVID ROCASTLE | – | ARSENAL |
| 17 | ALAN SMITH | – | ARSENAL |
| 18 | GARY LINEKER | – | FC BARCELONA |
| 19 | CHRIS WADDLE | – | TOTTENHAM HOTSPUR |
| 20 | JOHN BARNES | – | LIVERPOOL |
| 21 | PETER BEARDSLEY | – | LIVERPOOL |
| 22 | TONY COTTEE | – | EVERTON |

**England squad:**
Original list for the friendly against Greece in the
Olympic Stadium, Athens, February 8, 1989

# SNOD THIS for a LAUGH

# CHAPTER 1

# A WINFIELD WONDER

**My first steps towards professional football began with boots from Woolworths, a day-glo tracksuit and strict instructions from my dad**

*'Ian Snodin, a 16-year-old apprentice, came on as a substitute and showed coolness and class in his league debut to mark him as a player to watch in the future'*

**Match report, Doncaster 1-0 Bournemouth, 'So-Classy Snodin', 1980**

## ALL I WANT FOR CHRISTMAS IS…

WHEN I was 11, my Christmas wish list consisted of a football, boots, a kit and a tracksuit. In those days the 'in' teams were Leeds United, Manchester United and the local team, Rotherham United.

On Christmas morning, my brother Glynn and I would get up at two or three o'clock in the morning, open our presents and go back to bed. Of course we rewrapped them as best we could, trying to make it look as though they hadn't been touched. My mum and dad heard the footsteps but never said anything. When I opened mine, the ball was straightforward – it was just a basic case-ball. Then I opened the boots and asked: "What make are these?" Glynn started laughing and replied: "They're Winfield Wonders from Woolworths." I said: "Oh my God, I can't wear these." I put them to one side and picked out another parcel that I presumed were the kits. I opened it and saw a burgundy and blue top with a white neckline. I didn't even know whose kit it was.

I asked: "Who's this?" and he went: "Crystal Palace". I said: "Crystal Palace? Are they a team?" He replied: "Yeah, they're in the Third Division. That's the crest of an eagle. That's their nickname – Eagles." Then I opened the tracksuit – bright orange it was with a black stripe down the sleeve – Holland. I was horrified: "Oh my God – I've got Winfield Wonder boots, a Crystal Palace kit and a bright orange tracksuit."

We went back upstairs and came down later in the morning to pretend to open them in front of my parents. I asked the same questions of my dad that I asked Glynn earlier and protested: "I can't wear these." Dad told me: "Get them all on and get out there." I did as I was told and looked like the Tango man. I ran up to the school field behind our house to join my mates for a Christmas Day game. I could see all the lads in their brand new Adidas and Puma boots, Leeds United and Manchester United kits. They came running up to me and demanded to know: "What's that tracksuit?" I brazened it out: "Holland – don't you know your team?"

The football started and it was 20-a-side with me wearing bright orange. It was freezing initially but before long I was sweating cobs in this tracksuit. However, I daren't take it off because of the Crystal Palace kit underneath. Eventually I had no choice and all the lads came running up to me again. I told them that Palace were an "up and coming team". I was probably the best footballer so I didn't care what they thought – they all wanted me on their team anyway.

## "I WANT TO BE A FOOTBALLER"

I wasn't the best academically but always received sparkling reports in PE. I didn't take school work seriously and I wasn't pressured into revising. With the football, I always had Glynn to emulate. He played for the school and was part of Doncaster's youth team and I thought I could be better than him.

When I had my careers interview at 14 and was asked: "What do you want to do?" my reply was "footballer", which had been my goal from the age of seven. The fella who was talking to me tried to suggest I was being unrealistic but I wouldn't back down. The interview lasted about a minute.

## AN EXAMPLE TO FOLLOW

I was born and raised in Thrybergh, a mining village in Rotherham, South Yorkshire. My father, Colin, was a decent footballer. My mum, Elizabeth, is better known as Betty. According to all my dad's pals – and according to him – he was better than Glynn or I. Apparently he was a cracking player. He was wanted by Wolves, Burnley and Sheffield Wednesday but went off the rails through drinking and smoking. I think that's why he was quite strict with us in our football upbringing.

I saw first hand through Glynn what was required because he was three years older than me. I always looked up to him. My dad didn't allow him to go out to pubs and clubs. Glynn accepted this – he was more laid-back while I was a little bit fiery, but the rewards he was getting triggered me to behave myself.

Most of my mates became miners after we left school and

they earned good money compared to what I was on as a 16-year-old apprentice footballer. I had to travel on the bus from Rotherham to Doncaster so my money was taken up by bus fares, what I was having to eat and giving my mum board.

It was a tough upbringing. Dad was a miner himself so we were never flush with money and we never had a holiday abroad. We didn't feel deprived and I am grateful to my dad that he was strict. I needed that guidance. If I hadn't got that, I know for a fact that I wouldn't have been a footballer – I would have been a miner and gone out drinking with my mates.

## GROWING UP
Thrybergh was a close-knit community. Most of the men worked in the local mine, Silverwood Colliery. The working men's club was a focal point and all the parents socialised together. There would be annual coach trips to seaside resorts like Cleethorpes, Bridlington, Skegness and Scarborough. That was the highlight of the year because many of us couldn't afford a week's holiday, whether it was abroad or in Britain. It was very exciting to see 30 coaches lined up, waiting to find out which one you were on.

## BLUE IS THE COLOUR
As with most families in that era, the FA Cup final was a big thing in our house. We used to sit in the front room all day – Glynn, dad, mum, my younger sister Lisa and me. Curtains would be drawn from 9am onwards and the volume would be up. The cup final meant everything. The build-up started with breakfast with the players and, apart from toilet breaks, we would not move until the trophy had been presented. In 1970 when Leeds United played Chelsea I told my dad beforehand that whoever won would become "my team". It finished 2-2 and the replay was at Old Trafford two weeks later. The Londoners won 2-1 and I became a Chelsea fan.

They had a supporters' club in Rotherham and, when I reached 12 years old, I started to travel to Stamford Bridge on their coach. I used to go twice a season and I'd stand on 'The Shed' – the cheapest area of the ground. I was a massive fan and pictures of Peter Osgood and Charlie Cooke adorned my walls.

Funnily enough, I had a chance at 18 to sign for Chelsea after playing against them in a pre-season friendly for Doncaster. I was having a bite to eat with a couple of the lads when Ian Jones, the Doncaster chairman, called me over to his table, which he was sharing with his Chelsea counterpart, Ken Bates.

Ken said to me: "You're a good player, son. I've just been saying to your chairman that I'd like to buy you."

My shocked response was: "Well, I have been a Chelsea fan for most of my life but, if I'm truly honest, I don't think I'll join you."

"Why not?"

"I'm a northern lad. I've never been to London properly and I don't think I could handle it."

"No, you'll soon get used to it. I like what I've seen today and I would love to negotiate a deal with the chairman to bring you to Chelsea."

"I'm flattered but I'm a northern lad and I want to stay with my current manager. Thanks for the offer."

He was taken aback but I couldn't see myself down in London. A lot of players would have jumped at the chance but it wasn't for me. It was a completely different way of life and for me, from a mining village, it didn't appeal. I'm glad I didn't go; I don't think I'd have survived down there.

## ME AND MY BROTHER

Glynn and I were both very small as boys and the age group sides tended to go for bigger lads, who didn't have half the skill we possessed. Dad wasn't a pushy parent who couldn't handle rejection for his children, but he knew that we shouldn't have been overlooked.

Glynn travelled all over the place with Rotherham boys and only ever got on as a substitute for three or four minutes at a time. Dad let it go because Glynn wanted to be part of the squad but inwardly he was fuming. Eventually, towards the end of the season, his patience snapped and he pulled Glynn out.

When it came to my turn at 14 I sailed through the trials without a problem. I thought I was certain to play in the first game but I was made substitute. When I walked towards the bench before kick-off, I could see my dad shaking his head. The match was played and I didn't get on. Dad approached the manager afterwards and told him he was taking me out of the squad. I was gutted and protested but he insisted it was for my own good. People sometimes ask me if I played for England Schoolboys. I didn't even play for Rotherham Schoolboys.

Maurice Setters, who went on to be Jack Charlton's assistant with the Republic of Ireland, was the Doncaster Rovers manager who signed Glynn. I remember him arriving on our street in a big black Jaguar – nobody had a car like that round our way.

In he came and I was on the settee, colouring something in and not paying too much attention. I remember Maurice saying to my dad: "What's Ian like? Is he any good?" I looked up, carried on colouring and heard my dad say: "He'll be better than Glynn." Maurice joked: "Fucking hell, get another form out. Let's sign him now."

Of the two of us, I was more aggressive and could lose my rag with team-mates. Glynn was more skilful and used to go about his business in his own way. If he got kicked he used to pick himself up and get on with it, while I would argue and fight. I think he only got sent off once in his career, whereas I was sent off seven times. I could give a bollocking out to my team-mates whereas Glynn couldn't, although that's changed now he's become a coach.

I played for a local team in Doncaster called Edlington White Stars for one season when I was 14 and 15. Apart from that, it was just school football for me.

Stan Anderson was the manager of Doncaster by that stage and Glynn asked him if it would be alright for me to come in and train during the school holidays. He trained with the first team and I was with the schoolboys.

When I was 16 Rotherham asked if I would sign apprentice forms. I said no, even though they were my local team, because

I'd had two years training with Doncaster and got to know everybody. I felt comfortable there.

## THE BIGGER BOYS TOUGHEN ME UP

I used to play football twice a week with Glynn and his mates, who were three years older and considerably bigger than me. It made me harder as a person and mentally stronger. I could match them ability wise and learnt how to tackle and get stuck in. It was the same in school – at the age of seven, I was playing with 10 year olds. When I got into the Doncaster first team, I wasn't afraid because I was used to playing with older lads.

## A LESSON FROM DAD

When I was 15 and 16, I would have to be home by 10pm from the local youth club. On Friday nights dad wouldn't let me go out at all because of having a game the following day. He didn't want my performance to be compromised in any way.

In late January 1980, three weeks after I'd made it into the Doncaster first-team squad, I defied him and went to the youth club, while he made his regular trip to the pub for a couple of pints. I had two glasses of coke, a game of pool and a game of table tennis. Unfortunately, he came home from the pub early. I got back at 10pm and my mum told me he was already in. I froze on the spot.

He questioned me straight away.

"Where have you been?"

"The youth club."

"You know you don't go out on Friday nights."

"I've only had..."

"I don't care, you don't go out. What would Billy Bremner (then Doncaster manager) say if he knew you'd been out?"

"He's not going to find out."

"How do you know?"

The following morning I had a youth-team game at Edlington Miners Welfare Club, halfway between Rotherham and Doncaster. The first team were away at Bradford City that afternoon but Bremner always used to watch the youth team when he could. You respected the youth-team boss but when the first-team manager was there, you tried extra hard. We won 2-1 that day, I got both goals and played exceptionally well. Immediately after the game, Bremner said to me: "Come on, hurry up and get changed; you're coming with me to Bradford."

My dad had watched the game and left as soon as he heard I was joining up with the first team. I got in Bremner's car and as soon as I shut the door, he laid into me for going out the previous night. The bollocking didn't stop from leaving Doncaster until we arrived at Bradford. My old fella had told Billy what I'd done and asked him to have a word. I never did it again.

I'm glad my dad was like that because I was headstrong and a bit of a character. I could have gone down the wrong path if he hadn't been so strict.

# CHAPTER 2

'So much talent, it's almost frightening...'

WHEN Billy Bremner — 54 Scottish caps behind him and not a bad football judge — tells people he can show them the hottest property in English football they sit up and start to take notice.

But when he adds that the lad is playing in the Fourth Division with Doncaster Rovers, still only 20, and his name is Ian Snodin they tend to take it with a pinch of salt.

By Peter Catt

The only surprise for Bremner is that he has managed to hold on to him so long...

of the ways for both Bremner and his protege.

The Doncaster boss added: "I suppose you can't really stand in his way but we're pushing forward now and I'd love to build a...

# FAKE GOALS & FREE STEAKS

**A Doncaster player at 16, I looked like a choirboy and had to grow up quickly with Billy Bremner keeping me in line most of the time. As I began to make headlines, I developed a taste for the good life**

*'Ian Snodin looked the classiest player on the field yet still finished on the losing side...Doncaster's talented tactician was never out of his class even against Everton, the best team in England...he played like a modern Beckenbauer as he roamed across the field'*

**Sunday People, 'Classy Ian A Loser'**
**– Everton 2-0 Doncaster, 1985**

## A SECOND DAD

BILLY BREMNER, a Leeds United legend, became Doncaster's manager in 1978. In time, he became a second dad to me.

Even though I had been there for two years, we were still having trial games when I was in my final year at school in 1979. I didn't know whether I was going to be signed.

A lad called David Harle was amongst my group. He was born on the same day as me – August 15 1963. We were big buddies and celebrated our birthdays together; in fact, we are big mates to this day. He signed apprentice forms first so I went to see Billy, who told me they couldn't sign me until my 16th birthday. I pointed out: "You've signed Dave and we were born on exactly the same day." For some reason it took them another month to sort it out. I signed in August '79 and by the November I was in the first-team squad. My first game with them was at Hereford.

When I made my debut I was nine-and-a-half stone but Billy must have seen other things he liked. From then on, I never looked back.

## A BOLLOCKING FROM BILLY

In that summer of 1979, Dave Harle and I sneaked off to a little bookmakers when we were meant to be painting the old stand at Doncaster during the close season. There were tins and tins of paint delivered and it used to take us days to do. We got fed up and wandered off for a drink of pop and decided to have a bet. Because of our ages, we sent somebody in to put the bets on. I remember having £1 each way on two horses and they both came in. I won £164. That was eight weeks' wages because I was on £20 at the time.

We walked back eating ice creams, laughing and joking. I had given Dave £20 and we were buzzing. Suddenly Billy Bremner jumped out and gave us the biggest bollocking we'd ever had. He waited in the turnstiles for an hour until we returned. I was nearly in tears. A punishment awaited.

He said: "Right, I've just moved and we're having a house built. Tomorrow morning I'm taking you to my house. You are going to be shovelling sand from one end of the drive to the other." He did it to teach two mischievous kids a lesson.

When we arrived we saw a lorry dumping a vast amount of sand and our hearts sank, thinking we'd be there for days. He told his wife, Vicky, a lovely woman, that he would be back to pick us up at 4pm. He instructed her: "Just make sure they get a sandwich at one o'clock, a couple of cups of tea and that's it." She agreed: "Yes, alright William."

Off he went and I asked: "Any chance of a cup of tea, Mrs Bremner?" Vicky supplied us with two cups of tea, the biggest plate of chocolate digestives you've ever seen and told us: "Help yourselves." We sat down to tuck in but Billy had driven back. We were talking away, oblivious to him staring at us through the back window. He banged on the window and shouted: "Fucking work." We shit ourselves and jumped out of our skins. It was all planned and Vicky was in on it.

Billy was incredible to me. If I had any problems at home, if I'd done anything wrong, he'd be there to sort it out. I just worshipped him. I had a house built in Doncaster in the late 1990s which I called 'Bremner Lodge'. If I hadn't had him to guide me alongside my dad, I wouldn't have had a nice house and I wouldn't have been in football.

It was so sad when he died, aged only 54, in December 1997. I still used to ring him and see him when we were doing after-dinners. I was at my parents' one afternoon when there was a call from Peter Catt, who is the sports editor on the Doncaster Free Press newspaper. Dad, who was also close to Billy, answered the phone and I heard him say "oh, no". He passed it over to me and when Peter told me that Billy had suffered a heart attack and died, I couldn't speak for about a minute. I had tears streaming down my face.

We drove home with the kids in the back and I told my wife: "I'm going for a drink." I went to the snooker club, which was virtually empty, and stayed there all night before going back home at about six o'clock in the morning. I couldn't get over it for a good few months because he meant that much to me.

If you did the business for Billy, he'd do anything for you. He was an incredible fella. He gave me my debut at 16, made me Doncaster captain at 18 and within a day of him taking over at Leeds, he made me captain there by taking the armband off Peter Lorimer, his former team-mate.

He came with me when I went to talk to Everton and Liverpool. He just wanted the best for me. Even when I was leaving Doncaster and had a choice of West Brom or Leeds, he took me to see Johnny Giles, who was manager of West Brom, and Eddie Gray, who was managing Leeds. He didn't have any influence on my choice but he still looked after me.

I know a lot of people say he loved David Batty, the former Leeds midfielder, but I was his main kid. To this day I still see Vicky and she says "he absolutely adored you".

He saw in my game what he had in his: fiery, temperamental, a winner who hated getting beat. Billy Bremner had all that and he was world class. There are just not enough words that I can say about him.

## WINDING UP ALAN 'MAC'

The physio for the youth team and reserves at Doncaster was Alan 'Mac' McIvor, a great character who used to help the club on a part-time basis.

Billy Bremner used to enjoy winding him up. If we were leading comfortably and the game was in the final couple of minutes, he'd want one of us to fake an injury as far away from the dugout as possible. Mac, who loved his job, would sprint over as fast as he could to reach you. As he got within a few yards, you'd get up, put your arm up and say: "I'm alright." He would throw his bag and sponge to the floor and spit out: "You bastard." Everybody else would be in hysterics.

## ANOTHER BOLLOCKING FROM BILLY

Doncaster played Newcastle United in the FA Youth Cup shortly after I had broken into the first-team squad. The game ended in a draw and because the first team had no midweek game, Billy thought it would be good to bring Dave Harle and I back for the replay at St James' Park.

It was a freezing night, the coldest I'd ever played in, and the score was 0-0 early in the second half when I was sent off for retaliating following a bad tackle.

We eventually lost 2-0 after extra-time. In the dressing room afterwards I was sat with my head down. Bremner went round and shook every player's hand and said: "You were absolutely brilliant, outstanding tonight. There was only person who let you down so fucking blame him."

I knew who he was talking about as he began to address me: "Have a look at the sweat and disappointment on these young lads' faces. That is down to you. We brought you in to strengthen the team – we'd have been fucking better off without you."

I could feel tears rolling down my face. I knew he was right – I had let the lads down. It was a harsh lesson.

## COME IN, NUMBER 4

I made my first-team debut by coming on as a substitute when we played Bournemouth at home in March 1980. One of our players was injured and had to come off after an hour. As I was about to enter the pitch, I could sense the crowd were saying, "he looks about 12". Billy was player-manager and he assured me: "I'll look after you". He did exactly that, telling me what to do and where to go. I played one more game with him and then he dropped himself and gave me the number 4 shirt, which was a big thing as that had been his number. That was it, he never played again. From then on I made a big thing of getting the number 4 shirt at every club I played for.

## "DOES YOUR MAM KNOW YOU'RE OUT?"

I'd played a handful of games for Donny by the time we went to Aldershot in April 1980. Billy Bremner told me to get warmed up after about 70 minutes. I left the dugout and ran along the line, doing my stretches. All their fans were laughing at me because I looked about 12. One man shouted: "Fucking hell, he's a choirboy. Does your mam know you're out?" I turned around and it was a big, bearded fat fella, about six feet five inches. He was giving me absolute pelters. I didn't know how to react.

Eventually I came on and within two minutes the ball bounced to me just outside the 18-yard box. I took a touch and hit it – it flew in for the equaliser. My team-mates were after me but I thought: 'I'm going to find that big fat fuck with his beard.' Billy was stood by the dugout with his arms outstretched and I ran straight past him. I faced the big fat man and screamed: "She fucking knows I'm here now!" To be fair, the fella started clapping me and said: "Well done, son."

## A PAY-RISE REQUEST THAT ENDED IN GLORIOUS FAILURE
Aged 17, I was doing well for Doncaster and had been getting quite a lot of praise. At the time, I was earning £60 a week.

The captain, Alan Warboys, asked me how much money I was on. When I told him, he instructed me to ask Billy Bremner for a rise because I was now a first-team regular. I was reluctant to do so but he insisted.

When I went to Bremner's office that afternoon, I was dreading it. I had so much respect for him but there was plenty of fear as well. His secretary, Joan Oldale, pulled a face as if to say 'you're brave' when I told her what I was intending to do.

I knocked on his door and went inside.

"What can I do for you?"

"Gaffer, any chance of a rise?"

"You fucking what? Did I hear that right? A rise?"

"Yes, I'm in the first team now and a couple of the lads said I should be on more than £60."

"Get fucking out."

"What?"

"Get out."

I left his office and walked past Joan, who was tutting. Alan Warboys asked how I'd got on. When I told him what Bremner had said, he burst out laughing and said: "I was only winding you up. The boss always says: 'Never ask for a rise – a rise will always come to you.'" I'd been well and truly stitched up.

Shortly afterwards a phone call came through, asking me to see Bremner in his office. I walked in and he opened the conversation by asking: "When are you going to learn? Don't ever come to see me and ask for a rise. If you're doing the business on the pitch, I'll get you in and give you a rise."

About a week later he called me in and topped my wages up to £90 a week. When I signed a new contract at 18 he put me on £300 a week.

## GIVING SOMETHING BACK TO THE GRASS-ROOTS

While I played for Doncaster, I coached a young team known as Intake Boys. I used to take their training once a week and watch them play on a Sunday. Even though they were young lads, aged 10 and 11, I liked to give them an insight into what we would do and they were very successful. They all turned up to the registry office for my wedding in 1985 in their football kit, which was a lovely surprise.

I also helped a mens' team called Fullerton, although I was more involved in pre-season. They were mainly Glynn's mates and were three or four years older than me. I'd oversee the fitness training and join in with them. It was a good laugh and the only thing I didn't do was play with them on a Sunday.

They thought I had an easy life so I decided to give them a programme similar to what we had off Billy Bremner. Within 20 minutes they were moaning, groaning and throwing up.

I love grass-roots football. Even now, I get more satisfaction from watching kids playing on a Sunday than attending a Premier League game.

## DELIGHT AT PROMOTION

It was great to celebrate promotion from Division Four with such a small club in 1980/81. Towards the end of that season, Yorkshire Television's Calendar News programme filmed us in the dressing room before and after a game against Bradford. It was the first time I'd been up close in front of the cameras.

Billy Bremner told the interviewer, Martin Tyler, that although I was 17, he looked to me to run the show. I felt self-conscious and tried to duck out of the way of the cameras. We won 2-0 with goals from Steve Lister and Glynn and the dressing room was bubbling afterwards as we had nearly secured promotion. Occasionally I ask my dad if I can borrow his video tape of the Calendar feature to show my kids.

We were relegated in 1983 but bounced straight back up the following year. It was brilliant for a small town like Doncaster to be promoted. When you've got a successful team, it generates a great atmosphere; there is a buzz in the streets and the market. As a player, people notice you when you walk around and only have nice things to say – you might even get a free apple from the market. Whether you are at Manchester United or Morecambe, success for a football team lifts the spirits of everyone in the area.

## CAPTAIN AT 18

It was a big honour to be named Donny's skipper because there were lads in the squad with a lot more experience.

I vividly remember how it happened. I was cleaning my boots at 1.45pm before a 3pm kick-off when Billy asked: "Is everybody in?" I replied: "One minute gaffer." He shouted: "They should have been done fucking yesterday, not today. Get your arse in here." I put the boots down and shot in because you couldn't upset him. He spat "about time" and we all sat down. He went through the whole team and then said: "As you know, [Alan] Warboys is injured so we have a new captain for today – Snods." I sat back, 18 years old, looked at everybody and went: "What? You're kidding?" He said: "Do I look like I'm kidding you, skipper?" All the lads came up to me to offer their congratulations.

The first couple of times I was captain I thought it was simply a matter of tossing the coin up. I was scared to say anything to the experienced players initially but I grew into it; you become more confident and it makes you a better player.

I was always quite boisterous when I was growing up. One of the reasons Billy made me captain was to calm me down and make me act more sensibly. Unfortunately, the armband didn't always have that effect on me.

In one game at Swindon in December 1983, their number 6 was running the show. Billy Bremner shouted to me: "Wee man, sort out the number 6!" Within one minute I'd cleaned him out with the ball nowhere near. I was sent off and as I walked off I saw Bremner shaking his head in disgust. He angrily told me to get down the tunnel. When I protested that I was only following instructions, he yelled: "You had 70 minutes to sort it out – not 70 seconds."

The captaincy was a great honour and with it came responsibility. In a place like Doncaster you had to represent the club, opening bars or judging an Easter bonnet parade. When you are a small club, you need as much publicity as you can get. From a young age I was visiting schools. Glynn and I have decent names in the town and that's because we were good with the public and didn't get above ourselves. Billy Bremner and my dad wouldn't have allowed that anyway.

## "WELL DONE LIKE A PIECE OF COAL"
My dad used to have a roast dinner every day he came home from the pit, which would consist of Yorkshire puddings, potatoes, veg and the meat. Glynn and I would probably eat a roast three times a week, definitely on a Sunday without fail. We never went to restaurants – we couldn't afford it, simple as that.

In the early stages of my career I was looking through the Doncaster Evening Post and saw a full-page advert, which said: 'Local restaurateur Dennis Moullali offers any goalscorers for the Rovers a free meal.'

All the talk in the dressing room was about this offer. I happened to score in the next game and the lads said: "Why don't you go to Le Bistro and get the free meal?" I'd never really been anywhere so posh so this sounded exciting.

Accompanied by one of my pals, I introduced myself to Dennis who didn't have a clue who I was. I told him I'd scored and straight away he said: "Come in, son. Here's the menu." I looked through it and didn't have a clue what half the meals were. Eventually I chose a prawn cocktail to start and, for the main, the most expensive item on the menu, which was a fillet steak.

One of the waiters asked: "How do you want it cooked?" I didn't know what he meant so he explained: "You can either have it bloody, a bit pink in the middle or really well done like a piece of coal." I said: "Oh, yeah, I'll have it like that – really well done like a piece of coal. I don't want to see any blood."

I ate the prawn cocktail and my mate had a bowl of soup. The steaks came out and mine was just like I requested – a block of coal. I loved it and from that day on I've virtually always had well-done steak. It's only recently that I've felt brave enough to attempt medium to well-done.

After we got the bill I asked Dennis if we could halve it because I didn't want my mate to pay for his. He generously said: "Go on, you can both have it for free."

The following Saturday Doncaster were beaten. Dave Harle and I were talking about going for a couple of drinks and I said: "Fancy something to eat? We could go to that restaurant, Le Bistro." He went: "But none of us have scored," and I told him: "I went in there last week and the owner didn't have a clue I was a footballer." We decided to try it on.

When we walked in, Dennis greeted us: "Hi lads, can I help you?" He didn't recognise me. I introduced myself again and he remembered. "Oh, of course. How are you, son? Have you played today?"

"Yeah, we won 2-0."

"Did you score?"

"Yeah, and Dave got the other one."

Dennis called the waiter over and told him to get us a table. We both ordered fillet steaks. This carried on for four weeks. I took different lads and I made out I'd scored each time.

In the fifth week Willie Boyd, a goalkeeper, came with me. We had been beaten at Brentford but were starving on the way back so decided to try it on again, although we weren't convinced we'd get away with it.

It must have been getting on for 10pm by the time we went in because it was a long journey. Willie pretended to be a midfielder and they sat us down. There were more fillet steaks ordered and Dennis even bought us a drink each.

"Have a drink on me, lads. Great result."

"Thanks ever so much, Dennis."

Apparently, the next morning Dennis came downstairs in his dressing gown and slippers in his big house in a nice part of Doncaster. His wife was reading the paper and she asked how the night had gone. He told her I'd been in with "some fella called Willie Boyd who plays in midfield – they won 3-0".

She went: "I'm looking at the scores here and it says 'Brentford 1 Doncaster 0.'"

"What?"

"And Boyd is down as a goalkeeper. They've done you."

She called a neighbour who was a big Rovers fan who confirmed that I hadn't been scoring loads of goals in the previous few weeks.

We left it for a couple of weeks but the next time we went in, as soon as we got through the door, he was waiting for us.

"Fucking no chance."

"What?"

"You owe me fucking big time. You've only scored once in over a month."

We burst out laughing, he shook our hands and from that day I've been his pal – we regularly play golf together. He's got two nice restaurants in Donny that I'm always visiting.

## MEETING THE MISSUS

My wife Joanne and I celebrated our 25th wedding anniversary in July 2010. Her family owned a café in Doncaster's market place and that's where we met. The market used to be on a Tuesday, Friday and a Saturday and the traders would be in the café from 6am. Alan Warboys used to meet his wife there after training, so was a regular face. Joanne had seen a picture of us in the local newspaper and asked him who I was. Once he'd established that she fancied me, he told me about the young lass in the café and said he'd take me in one afternoon. When I went in and saw her, I thought 'very nice' and we set up a date.

There were no frills at our wedding. There weren't many people there, only close family, Billy Bremner, a few team-mates and the kids from Intake Boys who stood outside the registry office wearing their kit. It was lovely to see them. We married on a Saturday, had a nice meal and evening celebration and I started pre-season training on the Monday.

We are still together, over 25 years later. It's all Alan Warboys' fault.

## A 7-5 WIN AND A STOLEN MATCH BALL

During the 1982/83 season we played Reading at Belle Vue and won an incredible game 7-5. I scored my only career hat-trick, although two of them were penalties. Future England and Chelsea striker Kerry Dixon was playing for Reading and it was end-to-end, goals flying in everywhere. Kerry scored four himself.

At the end of the game, we were jubilant. I could hear the Reading manager giving them a massive bollocking and I thought: 'They're going to be in that dressing room for another 10 minutes.' I went to the referee's room and knocked on his door while the bellowing continued.

"Hi ref. Hat-trick?"

"You've come for the match ball? No problem, come in."

I grabbed it off him and quickly got all the Donny lads to sign it. Before long I could hear a commotion and the referee saying: "No, I've already given it to the Doncaster player."

Kerry came knocking on our door, asking if he could have the match ball. I held it up with all the Donny signatures and anecdotes and asked: "Do you still want it?" He was unimpressed: "Fucking cheeky..."

Later on, we were having a drink in the bar. Kerry shook my

hand and said, with a glint in his eye: "We'll cross swords again one day." We were having a laugh about it. That's how football was in those days, you used to have a drink in the players' lounge. Nowadays it's difficult to imagine both teams socialising together. They play the game and get on the bus straight away. When we were playing you used to kick hell out of each other for 90 minutes, go straight into the lounge, all mix and have a few drinks. That's missing now but if you talk to lads from my time, they'll tell you the players' lounge was the place to be. Now I think they are used as crèches.

## MUD AND THE MISSING BOOT

We played Rochdale at Spotland when I was 20, arriving at the ground after three or four days of torrential rain. There were seven big white buckets in the dressing room, catching the water that was coming through the roof. We had to go in, get changed and dodge all these buckets. We couldn't even warm up because the pitch was muddy as hell. I can't believe the game was played, even by the standards of the time.

I remember Glynn saying: "Surely referee, we can't play...the ball won't roll on here," but the official wasn't in the mood for a debate: "No problem, get on with it." After about 15 minutes I remember my boot flying off when I went to kick the ball. It was camouflaged in the mud and I couldn't find it. I must have spent a good minute running about this pitch in one boot and one sock while the game was going on. Eventually one of their players picked it up and held it up. I said "cheers, mate", at which point he lashed it down the other end of the pitch. I then had to run another 30 or 40 yards to finally retrieve the boot.

## INTEREST FROM LIVERPOOL

Shortly after he retired from the manager's job, Bob Paisley watched me on Liverpool's behalf when I was 20, which was phenomenal. I wouldn't say all players are affected by press cuttings but when you see yourself linked with what was then England's most successful club, it's very difficult to ignore.

After the story came out my performances dipped over a three-week period. You wonder if they're watching you; you try to do too much; you question whether you're too good to be at Donny. It did affect me until Billy pulled me into his office and told me to forget about everything and concentrate on playing. I knew that if it was the right time to leave the club, then he would have said so. I had that much faith in Billy Bremner that I'd do whatever he said.

## THREAT TO EMIGRATE

It would be more accurate to say I would almost always do what Billy said. There was one occasion when I defied him and acted stupidly because of youthful impetuosity.

By the summer of 1984 I had been in the England youth set-up for a while. Many of the lads in the squad had been in my ear, telling me that I should be playing at a higher level and earning more money. I wasn't bothered by material goods, money or flash cars but I wanted to play in a higher league. I knew I was as good as my England team-mates and I became frustrated that I wasn't competing at their level.

Doncaster had put a price tag of £200,000 on me which would have been a club record fee. I was captain but I thought it was too high. When nobody came in, I became frustrated and disillusioned. Stupidly, I went to Billy and told him I wanted to be placed on the transfer list. He tried to talk sense into me: "If anyone comes in for you, you will find out on the same day, even if you sign a new contract."

Despite this, I was headstrong and declared I was prepared to move to New Zealand, where my sister was staying with her then boyfriend. It would have been quite a step for a Yorkshire home boy like me. Bremner pointed out the flaws in my plan – there was no professional league out there so no obvious way of earning a living. Also, the club held my registration so I couldn't just walk away anyway. I kicked up a fuss and decided to stay away from training for a few days.

Billy rang me up and asked what I was playing at. He stripped me of the captaincy but once I returned I had it back after a few weeks. The more I think about it now, what a dick head I was. It was a two-week period of my life where I needed to grow up. I let Billy down, my team-mates and the supporters of Donny. After I'd calmed down, I eventually signed a new contract and 12 months later I was off to Leeds.

## FIRST GOODISON EXPERIENCE

The best feeling I ever had on a football field was at Goodison Park – when I played for Doncaster Rovers against Everton in the FA Cup fourth round in 1985. We must have taken 10,000 fans to watch us against the then best team in the country. I was in tears at the end of the game because our supporters were still singing. I've spoken about that match to Graeme Sharp, Kevin Ratcliffe, Peter Reid and Andy Gray and they can't remember it. For me, it was a memorable occasion.

## DEPARTING DONNY

I knew there was quite a bit of interest when I came to leave Doncaster in 1985. They still wanted £200,000 for me and two clubs said they'd pay the asking price.

It was between Leeds United and West Bromwich Albion. At the time, West Brom were in the First Division, managed by Johnny Giles. Leeds were a division below and Eddie Gray was player-manager. Billy said to me: "They were both my team-mates, they're both cracking fellas; the decision's yours."

He drove me down to West Brom; we were due there for 11am and arrived at 10.50. We announced ourselves at reception. At 11 Billy asked: "Can you get Mr Giles?" We were told he would be down in 10 minutes. Straight away Billy said: "Tell Johnny, Ian Snodin's in reception now. If he's 10 minutes we'll be back up the motorway." Within a minute Johnny Giles appeared.

He said to me: "Look Ian, I can show you round the ground – the directors' box, the lounge, the stands – but you aren't going to play in any of them." He took me to the dressing room, sat me down and spoke about figures and what he wanted from me.

He walked me down the tunnel to the pitch and told me: "That's your work." What he said made sense.

We left and went up to Leeds. Eddie Gray was waiting at the front door. He must have been desperate to make a good impression. Eddie showed me everything about Elland Road – there was a lot to see with their tradition and the trophies.

Leeds were my preference because it was only half-an-hour from Doncaster. I think I made the right decision because West Brom went down the following season with a very low number of points.

Glynn left Doncaster at the same time and went to Sheffield Wednesday for £150,000. I've got to mention Jimmy Lumsden, who is a coach at Everton now, because he was instrumental in me going to Leeds. Jimmy was often in contact with Billy Bremner and Billy would tell him how good I was. Without my knowledge, Jimmy became a regular visitor to Belle Vue and it was him who convinced Eddie to watch me a couple of times and then buy me.

After the talks with Leeds and West Brom, I knew my time at Doncaster was up. It was all I'd known since I was 14, catching the bus from Rotherham for training. I remember talking to Billy outside the ground; he shook my hand and I was in tears because of the affection I felt for Bremner, the club and the town. The last words I said to him were: "I hope our paths cross again and you become my manager once more." I wouldn't have long to wait.

# CHAPTER 3

# FLANNELS & CARRIER BAGS

**A move across Yorkshire meant I had to get up to speed quickly, although journeys into training proved hazardous. Before long I was reunited with Billy Bremner as we tried to revive Leeds United**

*'The best prospect for stardom is Ian Snodin...he reminds me of Bobby Moore or Jim Baxter, who both oozed confidence. I'm confident Snodin will be playing First Division football in the near future. From there he can become a major force in English football'*

**Press cutting, 'Snodin's Route To Stardom...' by Dave Hilley, 1986**

## SNODIN THE SPRINTER

IT was interesting signing for Leeds because I despised them as a kid. As I mentioned earlier, I became a Chelsea supporter when they won the 1970 FA Cup and from that point I fucking hated Leeds. They were known as 'Dirty Leeds' and were horrible as a team. I couldn't stand Billy Bremner when he played for them. I told him about my childhood feelings but he couldn't have cared less. Having said that, it felt great when I saw Elland Road on my first day.

One of the first things I did at my new club was take part in a sporting challenge – a sprint race against four of my team-mates.

In my last year at school I was reasonably quick but if there were eight in a sprint, I'd probably finish sixth. I started to grow when I was 17 and 18. Because I had no weight on me, I became fast. When I was 18, 19 and 20 I would have fancied myself to beat anyone in football in a race over a short distance.

When I signed for Leeds, Billy Bremner challenged Eddie Gray, then Leeds' player-manager, to a bet, claiming I would beat Terry Phelan, who was a whippet, over 100 metres.

The first day I was there we did a cross-country run, five miles around Roundhay Park. Eddie and Phelan took off like it was the 100 metres. I started laughing and said to Ian Baird: "What are they doing?" He replied: "They will keep that up for five miles." A seed of doubt grew in my mind and it wasn't long before the day of the race.

The competitors were Terry, Andy Linighan, Martin Dickinson, Roger Eli and myself. The assistant manager, Jimmy Lumsden, set us off with Eddie at the finishing line. I ran in my socks because I didn't feel comfortable in boots or spikes. Jimmy said: "On your marks; get set; go" and we were off. I was away like a motor vehicle and ran the last five yards backwards – I was that far ahead. Eddie said: "Fucking hell, Billy was right – you're a whizz."

## FREE-KICKS WITH LORIMER AND SHEZ-SHEEDY

The first league game of 1985/86 was against Fulham at Craven Cottage. We were awarded a free-kick 30 yards out, in the middle of the goal. There was nothing on when John Sheridan came over and said: "From 20 yards out to 40 yards out, 'Lash' takes everything."

Lash was Peter Lorimer, who I hadn't played with before. He came walking in off the touchline and I asked what the plan was. He was emphatic in his answer: "You're going to leave that ball and I'm going to hit it." The entire Leeds crowd were singing "90-miles-an-hour". I turned round to 'Shez' and said: "Are you sure?" Lorimer struck the free-kick; it went like a missile, hit the crossbar and flew into the area where our fans were gathered.

I had a lot of time for John Sheridan. When Colin Harvey was Everton manager, he was going to buy Stuart McCall. No disrespect to Stuart, but I tried to convince Colin to sign Shez instead. He was absolute quality in midfield.

I remember him being called up for the Republic of Ireland and coming back totally in raptures about Kevin Sheedy. All he kept going on about was "Sheedy, Sheedy, Sheedy".

In his first training session back, he said to me: "I've seen this free-kick...unbelievable. We should try it. You stand with your back towards goal, flick it up and I volley it. Sheedy does it." I was sceptical: "Shez, there's a difference between you and Kevin Sheedy." He was still keen though.

Billy Bremner (who replaced Eddie Gray as manager – see overleaf) started to run us through a routine and I butted in: "Gaffer: 'Sheedy' here's got one. He's seen something while he's been away with Ireland." Billy said: "Oh, this'll be interesting. Let's give it a go." We had 10 attempts and not one got within five yards of the goal. They went high, wide, into the car park, everywhere. I told him: "Shez, if you think I'm doing this tomorrow at Elland Road, you are very much mistaken."

Next day we were awarded a free-kick right in front of our Kop. Sheridan walked over and I could hear Bremner shouting: "Nooooooooo! No way. Put it in the box." Shez insisted on going through the routine we'd failed miserably at the day before – and straight into the top corner it went. He stood there with his hands in the air shouting: "Sheedy, Sheedy". The lads jumped on him, the crowd were going mad and Bremner was ecstatic. We won 3-1 and in the dressing room afterwards he was made up.

Sheedy and I went to watch boxing in Liverpool in early 2010 on a Friday night, and we called Shez at midnight to give him a load of abuse. He rung me the next day to complain because he was Chesterfield manager and they had a game on the Saturday.

## REUNITED WITH BILLY BUT DREADING THE CAPTAINCY

We struggled in my first couple of months at Leeds and Eddie Gray was sacked. I wasn't happy because he was one of the reasons I signed for them. I had a little bit to say to the chairman, Leslie Silver, and the directors. The lads who had been there longer than me were unhappy and I wanted to say my piece. I thought sacking him was unjust.

We heard rumours that Billy Bremner was coming from Doncaster and that softened the blow. I was upset that Eddie had gone but there was nobody better than Leeds' former captain and my former manager to take over. When I heard that he was being lined up, I phoned his house and Vicky answered. She said: "He's told me not to say anything to you; he knew you'd be ringing up." Within two days he was the new manager.

As pleased as I was about that, I was dreading him taking the captaincy off Peter Lorimer, a Leeds legend, and giving it to me. I'd only just gone there and with him being my former boss, I didn't want the players thinking of me as his blue-eyed boy.

On his first or second day, I was sat in the dressing room getting changed when I heard one of the coaching staff come through and say: "Peter, the gaffer wants a word with you." Deep down, I was thinking: 'No, please don't do it; it's too early.'

After a few minutes Peter came back in and said to me: "The gaffer wants you." I knew. As I was walking to his office, I was thinking of the lads because I thought they'd hate me.

Billy said: "Sit down, son. You're the new captain of Leeds United." I pleaded with him: "Gaffer, don't. Not yet." He said: "I want you as the captain of my team. I've had Peter in and he's totally accepted it. He thought that if I was going to give it to anybody, you were the right person. You're a winner. Don't think it's too early; I'm the manager and you're the club captain."

I felt embarrassed but when I walked back into the dressing room, Peter came straight up to me, shook my hand and said: "Congratulations, son." All the other players followed suit. The warmth I received was generous and very reassuring.

## YOUNG TALENT

When I joined Leeds, we had some talented young players. Denis Irwin and Scott Sellars were 19, while John Sheridan was 20. Sheridan was from an Irish family in Manchester and had a nasty streak; he could handle himself on the pitch. Denis was very quiet and shy; Scott was similar – frail and quiet but with great ability.

In one of Billy's first games as Leeds manager he saw Andy Linighan put a gumshield in his mouth. He wasn't impressed and told Andy to take it out. I think Bremner decided then to get rid of him – he wanted his centre-halves to have broken noses and cauliflower ears.

Billy made big mistakes in letting Linighan, Sellars and Irwin go in 1986. He should have shown more patience. He felt they weren't strong characters but they had only just turned 20 and were terrific footballers. Linighan and Irwin went to Oldham and blossomed before moving on; Andy eventually to Arsenal and Denis to Manchester United. Sellars was an important player for Blackburn Rovers.

David Batty and Gary Speed were apprentices when I was at Leeds. You could tell they were going to be great players. When Batty was 16, he looked the spitting image of me when I was that age, small with a pudding bowl haircut. He also had a devilment on the pitch and Bremner loved that.

That devilment was demonstrated during a practice match between the first team and a mix of reserve and youth players. Batty was in the centre of midfield and went over the top in a tackle with John Sheridan. Shez grabbed him around the neck and screamed: "If you ever do that again, you little bastard, I'll kill you." As I watched this, I thought 'that was me when I was 16'. Batty didn't react or utter a word. Five minutes later, the same thing happened. Sheridan really went for him and I had to stand in between them. I had a quiet word with Batty and told him not to lose the aggression from his game, but explained that such tackles on your team-mate in training were not on.

## GET ME A F***ING FLANNEL

With the help of a £500-a-week contract and a car allowance, I bought a Mitsubishi Colt for my Missus for £1,000. For weeks on end I went on about how nice it was.

I had to take it into training one day when it was my turn to pick up my team-mates Ian Baird and John Buckley. As we pulled up at Baird's house, the reaction was: "Woah, is this the car then? Is this 'The Grand'?"

We were driving down the motorway to Elland Road when, to my alarm, I noticed the temperature gauge was high. We still had another 25 minutes to go and I was thinking about the stick I was going to get. When I pulled up, Baird and Buckley were laughing their heads off – all they kept saying was: "Oooh, isn't it great for a grand!"

We were on the hard shoulder, about half-a-mile from the slip road at Barnsley. I lifted the bonnet and went to release the tap to let off a bit of pressure when hot, steaming water blew up in my face, taking the skin off. My face was on fire. From a laugh, it was now very serious.

The three of us were desperately trying to flag a car down but none stopped. I was running up the hard shoulder shouting: "Get me a fucking flannel, my face is on fire!" We reached the top of the slip-road and, luckily, there was a police car parked up. The officer inside took us straight to Barnsley Hospital while I stuck my head out the front window so cold air would blow on me. I could hear Baird and Buckley sniggering in the back and I was still shouting: "Fucking hell, get me a flannel!"

When I got to the hospital, a nurse said to me: "We're just

going to put a bit of cream on your face." I shouted: "Fucking cream. I don't want any fucking cream, I need a flannel." She replied: "No, no, it'll be no good. We've got to put antiseptic cream on."

They took me up to a ward, gave me a couple of tablets and I settled down. I was in there for three days. My wife didn't even recognise me when she arrived because my face was so burnt. I was very lucky because I could have been blinded.

I was back training a few days later. As I arrived, there was a sign on the dressing room door: "Get me a fucking flannel." When I walked in, there were about eight flannels hanging from my peg. Above them was another sign: "You wanted a flannel; we've got you a fucking flannel." That's the way football is. In any other walk of life, there would have been concern and sympathy. You have to grow up very quickly in a dressing room.

## A CARRIER BAG ON THE HEAD ON A COLD DAY

There was another comedy incident involving a trip into training at Leeds United. My mate Dave Harle had joined us from Doncaster and on this particular day it was his turn to drive us in.

Dave took his dad's car, a Ford Granada. It was November-December-January time and freezing – a severe frost, probably minus three. He picked me up and then we went for Ian Baird. As we were about a mile away from Baird's house, a pebble flew up, hit Harle's windscreen and shattered it. It was a case of: 'We've got to get to work. What are we going to do?' Bairdy came out of his house and saw the damage but his wife had already left with his car so switching vehicles wasn't an option.

Dave Harle had a plan: "Just get me a hammer. I'll smash the window out." I was aghast: "What? We're going to drive for half-an-hour without any windscreen in this weather? Harley, no fucking chance."

Bairdy brought out his hammer and the whole windscreen was knocked out. Then Dave asked: "Bairdy, have you got a carrier bag in your house?"

"Yeah, no problem."

Dave put the bag over his head, made holes for his eyes and sellotaped it around his neck. We were pissing ourselves. His dad had left his sheepskin coat in the back of the car so we huddled underneath it. We were going along the M1 to Leeds from Rotherham at 80 miles an hour, in the outside lane, it was minus three and the carrier bag was rattling. People were looking at us with mouths wide open, pointing in disbelief.

When we arrived, Dave couldn't get his hands off the steering wheel and his eyes were ice blue. I unravelled the sellotape to get the bag off his head. He was frozen. We had to thaw him out for a good hour – we ended up putting him in the sauna.

## ORMSBY LEAVES NOTHING TO THE IMAGINATION

For a Christmas party when I was at Leeds, we took our costumes to training and changed into them afterwards. We began by heading to a pub called The Peacock, which was close to Elland Road, with me dressed up as Worzel Gummidge. We moved on to a snooker club owned by Joe Johnson, who was world champion in 1986, before we did some pubs in town. Eventually there were half a dozen of us left in a nightclub at 1am. We were all drunk but defender Brendan Ormsby, wearing a Roman costume, was the only one on the dancefloor.

Towards the end of the night, Ian Baird ran over and led me to Brendan – people had just noticed that he had no underwear underneath his Roman dress. He was lifting the dress up and the women present were very excited. His manhood was a fair size so he had every reason to flaunt it.

## ON CRUTCHES AND IN MID-AIR

We played Bradford City at the Odsal Stadium early in the 1986/87 season, before they moved back to Valley Parade following the appalling fire in May 1985. At the time only Leeds United members were allowed to go to away games because there had been trouble involving the club's supporters. For over a season, they had been allocated limited numbers of tickets for away matches, generally 1,500-3,000 at the maximum. The ban was lifted before the game at Odsal and there must have been 7-8,000 from Leeds who made the short journey.

After five minutes I went up for a header. As I landed I could feel something wrong with my knee. I carried on for a couple of minutes and then called the physio over. I was banging my foot on the floor but the physio said: "No, no. Don't do anything – you're coming off. I think you've torn your cartilage." Unbeknown to me, Everton manager Howard Kendall was there to watch me and Ron Yeats was present too, scouting me for Liverpool.

I changed, was strapped up and given crutches. The facilities at Odsal were quite basic and they had portable dugouts. I hobbled out and sat in the portable cabin with Billy Bremner, the coaching staff and the physio while I waited for an ambulance to take me to hospital. Suddenly, I heard a big bang behind me. Leeds fans had set the cap fire and started rolling it down the terraces. Then they invaded the pitch and went straight for this portable dugout. They lifted it up with us all still sat in it. I was in mid-air holding my crutches and they were singing: "We are Leeds, we are Leeds, we are Leeds." I was convinced I was going to fall off from this great height but they eventually brought us back down to earth. Soon afterwards the ambulance arrived and I couldn't get out of there quick enough. Howard Kendall told me months later that when he saw the Leeds' fans invade the pitch, he thought: 'What a scouting mission this is.'

## HIDING IN THE BOOKIES

Before I was faced with the dilemma of joining Everton or Liverpool, Sheffield Wednesday attempted to sign me. Mick Hennigan, who was assistant to their manager Howard Wilkinson, was the man tasked with persuading me to move to Hillsborough. Glynn was at Wednesday himself at the time and had told me how Wilkinson used to run the bollocks off them in training. I didn't fancy any of that.

I found Mick waiting at my house when I returned home from training. His was car on the driveway – a sponsored vehicle with 'Mick Hennigan – Sheffield Wednesday' written all over it.

SNOD THIS FOR A LAUGH

I turned my car around and drove off. I kept phoning Joanne to see if he was still there. When she was talking to me, she had to avoid making it obvious that it was me on the phone. She was losing patience: "Get your arse back here – he's had eight cups of tea. Just tell him you don't want to sign for him." Eventually he left after three-and-a-half hours after talking nothing but football. I was in the bookies in town having a bet.

## THE LEAVING OF LEEDS

After only 18 months, I didn't want to leave Leeds United. I was captain, idolised the manager and the fans loved me.

I found out that the Liverpool player-manager, Kenny Dalglish, was interested and then I discovered Howard Kendall was also in for me on Everton's behalf. A reporter rang me about it and I told him: "I don't want to leave Leeds, I love it here."

I believe the first offer to the board was £650,000 and I told Billy Bremner that I didn't want to go. Within two days the offer was £750,000 and I repeated what I'd already said. Billy was satisfied: "That'll do me, I've told the board I want to build a team around you to get us back in the First Division." Two days later the offer was £850,000 and this time it wasn't Bremner who came to see me, it was the chairman, Leslie Silver. He came up to me with the vice-chairman and said: "Look, Ian, Everton and Liverpool have bid £850,000." Before I could get a word out, he added: "Take your pick, you're fucking going." It was great money for them and a great move for me, although I didn't see it like that at the time. It allowed them to buy new players and also to pay off a debt.

I went to watch Leeds in the FA Cup semi-final against Coventry at Hillsborough later that season. My dad was with me and a few fans started calling me Judas. I couldn't get my head around that. I gave everything for them and didn't want to leave. I was absolutely fuming – if only they knew the truth. I've been to loads of Leeds functions since and told that story so hopefully people know now. I had a great time there, it's a brilliant club with brilliant fans, but it was time to move on.

# CHAPTER 4

# SOCIAL CLUB

In 1987 I joined Everton, a team who could play hard on and off the pitch, rejecting Liverpool in the process. I came across some unique characters, including Gazza, Psycho Pat and Magnum

*"The lads had been pulling my leg that I had only scored against Third and Second Division teams in cup-ties, so it was nice to open my account. To be honest, I've never been much of a goalscorer, and I would be very happy with eight in a season"*

**Ian Snodin, Newcastle United 1-1 Everton, October 1987**

## EVERTON OR LIVERPOOL?

IT was exciting to read the speculation in the press about which team I was going to sign for. If you pick up a newspaper and see yourself targeted by the best two clubs in England, and probably Europe, you think: 'I'm nearly there. I must be a half decent player.'

I was quite content living in Donny and playing for Leeds United but once the chairman told me I had to go, I was clear in my mind that it was now Liverpool or Everton. Jo left the decision entirely up to me as she always accepted that being married to a footballer can mean moving around.

The talks were organised through Billy Bremner with no agents involved. He arranged for me to meet Howard Kendall at 2pm on a Monday in Blackburn, and Kenny Dalglish at 7pm later that day in Burnley. I don't know why they wanted to meet in those locations but I was happy enough with it.

After training at Leeds that morning, we travelled to Blackburn where we met Howard and Jim Greenwood, the Everton secretary, in a hotel conference room. I spoke to them while Billy waited in reception.

Howard and Jim told me how I'd fit into the team, how they'd been watching me and how much they wanted me. They were desperate for me to sign there and then and that was a great feeling. If Billy hadn't been there, I'd have probably done so, but I said I'd need to speak to my manager and he needed to see the contract.

I showed Billy what they were offering and told him they wanted me to sign straight away. He looked through the contract and made changes where he wasn't happy with certain details. Billy then led me back into the room and took charge: "Right, Howard, Jim: I'm not happy with that...that can come out...he wants this...and he won't be signing here today. He's going to see Kenny Dalglish in Burnley later." I think Howard and Jim believed they were going to lose out.

We had a cup of coffee and a sandwich and went to a hotel in

Burnley to meet Kenny, Peter Robinson, the Liverpool club secretary, and Sir John Smith, the chairman. Again, Billy waited outside. Kenny didn't really say a lot, it was Smith and Robinson who were doing all the talking about figures. I was a bit in awe – I was only 23 and on my own with big people in football.

Kenny then asked the other two to leave because he wanted to discuss football. He opened by saying: "Whatever they said, if you want more money, ask for more money." I explained: "Kenny, it's not about money. I'm not interested and have never been driven by it." He responded: "I'll give you more money than that. I want you at my club." It was a case of, 'Oh my God, what am I going to do?' I told Kenny: "I need to think about this."

Again, Kenny was pushing me to sign there and then. I went down to speak to Billy and told him: "My head's a shed at the minute. It was about 10.30 p.m.                                       home.

Billy led me back in and said: "Kenny, absolutely brilliant, thanks very much. Thank you Mr Smith, Mr Robinson, but Ian needs time to think about this overnight. It's not a simple decision and he doesn't want to rush into it." The response was: "Yeah, completely understand. No problem."

We drove home and my head was everywhere. I was thinking 'Kenny Dalglish, absolute legend; Howard Kendall, what a team they've got.' Billy explained they wanted a decision by midday the following day. He told me to come in for 11am to sort it out.

I went home, took a sleeping tablet and told Joanne what the circumstances were. They'd doubled my wages but I didn't know what to do. I slept well, got up the next morning and my Missus asked: "Who's it going to be, then?" I said: "I don't know. The first you know will either be on the radio or if I get to phone you up."

I left the house at 10am. Apparently, 15 minutes later the phone rang and it was a journalist trying to find out whom I was going to sign for. He was offering Joamme money if she could tell them. She said: "You are not going to believe this but he doesn't know."

I went in and met the gaffer at 11.15.

"Well?"

"I still don't know."

"You'd best fucking hurry up, son. You've got 45 minutes."

It got to 11.55 and I knocked on Billy's door, walked in and announced: "I've made my decision. Everton."

He didn't ask me anything other than to say: "Are you 100% sure?" As soon as I said "yes" he shouted his secretary: "Maureen, can you get me Howard Kendall on the phone, please?"

The call came through and he picked up the phone: "Howard, I've got the lad with me now." He put me on and, from the tone of Kendall's voice, I'm sure he expected me to sign for Liverpool.

He opened: "Yes, son?"

"I just want to tell you I've thought about it and made my decision."

"Yeah, what is it?"

"I'm coming to join you."

"You what?"

"Yes, thanks for the offer, I'd love to join you: I want to sign for Everton Football Club."

"Oh, I'm absolutely made up. Are you sure?"

"100% sure."

"What time can you get here? I want you to train with us this afternoon."

"It'd probably take an-hour-and-a-half."

"Get here for 2pm. We'll have your medical and we'll go down and see the press at Goodison to announce you as an Everton player."

I put the phone down. You could tell he was absolutely buzzing. I went to leave the room and Billy Bremner inquired: "Where are you going?"

"I've got to get a few things ready and then I need to get over to Merseyside to train with Everton."

"No, you are phoning Kenny Dalglish and telling him you are not signing for Liverpool."

I looked at him pleadingly and said: "You're fucking joking."

"No, you are going to be a man about this. Phone Kenny now."

Thinking of telling Kenny Dalglish that you are not going to sign for him was very scary. I pleaded: "Gaffer, will you do it for me?"

"You're doing it. Maureen, get me Kenny on the phone."

I went from elation at telling one manager I was signing for him to being petrified at the thought of speaking to the one I had rejected. I was shaking. It wasn't long before we got the message from Maureen and Billy picked up the phone.

"Hey, Kenny. I've got Ian with me." I could hear his voice and he was dead bubbly. He clearly thought I was going to sign.

I opened up: "Hiya, Kenny."

"Hiya, son. How are you?" It was a totally different reaction to Howard.

"Yeah, I've made my decision, Kenny, but I'm going to sign for Everton."

"You're fucking joking."

"No."

"You can't be. Please change your decision. I will drive up now to Leeds to meet you and I'll treble the money we've offered you. I want you at Liverpool Football Club."

"I can't do it, Kenny, I'm ever so sorry. I think you are a top, top man but I've already phoned Howard and told him I'm signing and I'm not going to go back on my word. I've made my decision."

"Is Billy there?"

I couldn't wait to pass the phone over. I shot out of the room and left the two of them to talk. Billy eventually came out and said: "He can't believe it."

I drove over the Pennines to sign for Everton and couldn't work out what was going to happen. I found Bellefield okay, although I had to ask for directions a couple of times along the way. One was from a lady and then I asked a fella. He looked at me and said: "Snodin, isn't it?" He shook my hand and added: "Come on the blue boys."

I felt excitement rather than pressure. I felt great that I was signing for a big club and wasn't fazed by the media attention. There was a disappointment that I'd left Leeds but I was joining a great team with excellent players. There are many good players who have never won a championship medal, as I did in my first season.

## "THE BOSS IS NOT HAPPY WITH YOUR DRINKING"

When Leeds attempted to sign Asa Hartford in 1971, they found he had a hole in the heart. Subsequently, when I signed for them in 1985 I had to undergo a two-day medical. I saw a knee specialist, an ankle specialist, a back specialist, I had my blood taken at the hospital, and I had my heart monitored. It was nothing if not thorough. It was a bit different at Everton.

I arrived at Bellefield and Howard told me how delighted he was. Then he said: "This medical, a formality. You've turned them down to join us, they'll not really be a medical. Just go into the back room and the club doctor will be there along with the physio. Within an hour we'll be at Goodison."

When it started I remember the doctor said: "Strip off, son." I took my minging tracksuit off and was stood in my undies. He turned around and said: "He looks fit, Howard." Then he asked: "Ian, can you get on the bench?" I did so and the doctor said: "He's agile." I thought: 'Fucking agile? What's all this?'

He checked my knee and ankle, pressed on my back and turned to Kendall again. "That's it then, Howard. No problems here." It must have lasted 10 minutes. I thought: 'This can't be it, surely?'

Howard then said: "Doc, what about the questions you have to ask him?" The doc opened his briefcase while Kendall carried on talking: "Don't you think you're rushing this a bit, Doc?" I was sat on the bench, nervous as a kitten.

Then the doctor asked: "Any illnesses in the family, Ian?"

"No, not at all."

"Do you smoke?"

"No, I've never touched a cigarette in my life."

"Do you drink?"

"In moderation, doc."

"What's moderation?"

"Just after a game, maybe five or six pints."

He started making notes and muttered to himself in a concerned manner. Howard asked: "Can I have a word, doc?" The two of them walked off to the corner of the room. I was thinking: 'My God, what have I said? I should have said one pint, not five or six.' The conversation seemed to last five minutes but it was probably only 20 seconds. They came walking back and the doctor said: "The boss is not happy with your drinking." I must have turned white.

Howard said: "Five or six pints a week...hey son, if you want to sign for this club today, you had better treble the amount you're drinking. We can fucking play on the field and we can play off the field. We love a social here – that's the team spirit we've got."

I looked at him in shock and said: "To be fair Mr Kendall, I do like a drink."

"Don't worry, son. I've had you checked out. I know you love a social. Now come on, let's go down to Goodison – you're an Everton player."

We headed to Goodison and news of my signing was all over the car radio. There were about 10 kids hanging around by the ground and they started shouting: "Go 'ed, Snowy!" I'd never been called Snowy in my life but it soon caught on. There were a couple of Reds shouting: "Wrong choice – you'll learn." Then there was another fella: "Snowy. Go 'ed, lad! Best club in the world but do yourself a favour – shave that fucking muzzie off and get that mullet cut." I started laughing, went inside, met the press and that was it – I was an Everton player.

## WHY I MADE THE RIGHT DECISION

I had studied Liverpool's team and they had Craig Johnston and Ronnie Whelan out wide. I looked at the two central midfield players, Steve McMahon and Jan Molby, and thought: 'I ain't going to get in there.'

I looked at the Everton team and the two wide midfield players were Trevor Steven and Kevin Sheedy. I wasn't going to replace them, which I was delighted about, because I hated playing on the wing. The midfield duo were Peter Reid, getting on a bit but still a brilliant player, and Paul Bracewell, who was injured. I considered everything and thought: 'I've got a chance of getting in there straight away.' That's why I went for Everton; I just didn't think that I'd get in Liverpool's team at the time.

People have said: "You must regret your decision." Fine, Liverpool won a few more trophies but I can honestly say that because of the way I've been treated by the fans, by everybody associated with the club, I would still choose Everton. It probably would have been the same at Liverpool but that doesn't matter. Everton have looked after me.

## AN INTRODUCTION TO THE EVERTON WAY

I used to wear whatever I wanted at Leeds: jeans with holes, tracksuits with holes; nobody cared. When I got to Everton and thought of the players there – Graeme Sharp, Kevin Ratcliffe, Peter Reid – I decided I needed to wear my best gear. I remember putting on a pair of dark blue trousers and a sweater before going into Bellefield.

When I arrived, the lads were relaxing and having a laugh before training. There were a couple of photographers present to take some pictures of me. Adrian Heath caught sight of me and said to Kendall: "Fucking hell, Howard. Who dressed him? Take him to town this afternoon and buy him some proper clothes." I asked: "Why? What's up with it?" and Adrian said: "You're not going to survive in Liverpool if that's your best gear."

I couldn't play against Southampton in the FA Cup third round on the Saturday because I'd not signed in time. Instead, I played head tennis on the morning of the game with the lads who were coming back from injury. Reidy was out of action at the time and he was tasked with taking me for lunch. The lunch turned out to be a sandwich and five or six pints of lager at a pub on Queens Drive in Liverpool. After about five pints, I was thinking 'I'm getting pretty tipsy here.' I was half-pissed by the time I got to the ground to watch the match. Howard greeted me, put his arm around me and asked: "Nice lunch?"

"Yeah, it was alright, thank you."

"What did you have?"

"A nice sandwich and five or six pints."

"Just what you told me when you signed."

## OPPOSING MY BROTHER

My Everton debut came at Goodison just over a week after I signed in January 1987. The opponents were Sheffield Wednesday and in their team was a certain Glynn Snodin.

Mum turned up that day. I was a substitute and desperately wanted Glynn to do everything right, while at the same time wanting my new team to win. It was quite difficult to watch while also wondering if I was going to get on.

Howard told me to warm up when we were 2-0 up. As I did so, I was given a great ovation and that must partly have been because I'd turned down Liverpool. When I came on, I ran around but wasn't able to do much. One of the reports said I showed some classy touches but that was an exaggeration. The game was a blur and I didn't really touch the ball but I knew deep down there was a lot, lot more to come from me. It was just great to be on the same pitch as my brother – we'd both made it to the top, playing First Division football. There couldn't have been anyone prouder than our parents. We'd come a long way from me having my orange tracksuit, Crystal Palace kit and Winfield Wonder boots.

## MY FIRST DERBY EXPERIENCES

Four days after my Everton debut, we played Liverpool at Goodison in the League Cup quarter-final. I was dreading seeing Kenny Dalglish. I walked down the tunnel before the game and, almost inevitably, he was the first person I saw. In fairness, he walked right up to me, put his hand out and shook my hand. He said: "Hey, Ian. All the very best, son. I believe you made the wrong decision but you're a good player and that's why I wanted you."

Every time I see him he always reminds me. I played in the Marina Dalglish charity game at Anfield in 2006, and, before the game, Kenny collected signatures from the Everton players. Sharpy was sat next to me and said: "Kenny, he didn't sign for you in '87, he's not going to sign for you now." I get on famously well with Kenny. He could have been an arsehole over it but he was anything but.

I started my first derby game at Anfield in April '87, just before we clinched the league championship. The tension in the dressing room beforehand was something I'd never witnessed. The lads were so pumped up and were banging on the walls, shouting: "Come on, let's get into them." I could hear exactly the same thing going on in the Liverpool dressing room.

The game kicked off, I turned to the referee, asked how long had gone and he said: "18 minutes". I'd not even had one kick of the ball. About two minutes later I got my first touch and Steve McMahon came through me at thigh-high. I was flat out but I remembered what Reidy had told everybody before the game: "If you get injured, you don't fucking show them." Jan Molby came up as I lay down and mimed blowing smoke from a cigar. He said to McMahon: "He turned down a chance to sign for us. We didn't want him anyway – he's shit." I was in a lot of pain but I got up. You can't have a better feeling than playing in an Anfield or Goodison derby.

## MY FIRST GOAL, MISSED BY DAD

I was in the starting XI for an FA Cup fourth-round tie at Bradford. I got a complimentary ticket for my dad and his mate as I wanted him to be there. This was going to be a first for him because he had never watched either of us play professionally since he attended a reserve game where Glynn came in for quite a bit of stick, which upset him. He always said he'd be too nervous anyway.

I was made up that this was going to be the first time he saw me play since my youth team days. During the warm up I saw him and thought, 'My God, I can't believe he is here.' I gave him the thumbs-up. The game kicked off and I was getting loads of stick every time I touched the ball. The Bradford player John Hendrie turned to me and said: "The only way to shut all these up is by scoring a goal."

After 25 minutes I looked up and my dad was still sat there. I thought he was doing unbelievably well. Early in the second half Adrian Heath picked up possession and I made a run into the box; the ball came across and I sent a diving header into the top corner. It was right in front of the Everton fans so I picked myself up and jumped onto the railings in front of them. They were going absolutely wild and I was thinking, 'It doesn't get much better than this.'

I ran along the line to see my dad but only saw my dad's mate, who shrugged his shoulders. Dad had left and was in his car listening to the radio commentary. I was gutted and for the next five minutes I couldn't concentrate on the game.

I had a drink in the players' lounge afterwards, went to my car and he was sat there in the passengers' seat. He shook my hand and said: "Good goal then, mate."

"I can't believe you left."

"But they were saying it was a good goal on radio."

## NAKED IN BORDEAUX

We played a friendly in Bordeaux shortly after I signed, which we won 2-1. We went out on the lash afterwards.

I scored and celebrated as though it had been the winner in the European Cup final. Before I knew it, I was absolutely plastered. I was rooming with Alan Harper and eventually I said to him: "I need to go to bed, Al." I remember him and Kevin Ratcliffe taking me to bed and laying me out.

I woke up in the night and felt absolutely freezing. I leant over to pull the quilt over my body and grasped thin air. I thought, 'Where is it?' I was groping desperately for this quilt and as I did so I heard a bell ring. I opened my eyes and an old couple emerged from a lift in front of me.

Harper and Ratcliffe had carried me out of my room completely naked and laid me on a settee right outside the lift. I looked up and the old lady, who was English, exclaimed: "Oh my God! I've seen some sights but nothing ever like this." I put my hand over my manhood, stood up and spluttered an apology: "I'm ever so sorry." She replied: "It looks alright from where I'm standing." I ran back down the corridor to my room, completely starkers. It was a case of 'Welcome to Everton'.

## MAGNUM'S CAMEO TURN

When I joined Everton the physio was big John Clinkard, a Tom Selleck lookalike known as 'Magnum'. John was a bit of a character and was even invited to open a bar dressed as the Hawaii TV detective.

A few weeks into my Everton career I picked up a slight groin strain and went for my first treatment from him. He was using the ultrasound machine and chatting away to me when 'Word Up' by Cameo came on the radio. He immediately put the ultrasound into its holder and started singing along, doing all the moves from the video and holding his bollocks. He carried on for the whole song. As soon as it finished, he sat down, picked the machine up and carried on as though nothing had happened.

## BARNEY WITH SHARPY

When I first arrived at Everton, I travelled to and from Yorkshire a great deal. My form on the pitch was indifferent and Graeme Sharp had a go at me – he wasn't happy that I was based in Doncaster and didn't spend much time with the players after games. It was a proper slanging match and we nearly came to blows. The following day he apologised but I realised he had a point. From that point, we became big pals and I made an effort to socialise more.

## ENCOUNTERS WITH MR WHITEHURST

Billy Whitehurst, a fearsome striker, was the hardest player I came across in football. I first met him when I was 17 and Doncaster had an FA Cup tie at Hull City. An hour-and-a-half before kick-off, the players were studying the pitch, deciding what type of boots to wear. Billy Bremner was talking to Whitehurst and the gaffer called me over. He introduced me and told him that I was going to be a top player.

Whitehurst said: "If he says you're going to be a top player, then you definitely will be a top player because he was unbelievable. I love him to death. All the best for your future, Snods."

I shook his hand and said: "Cheers, Billy."

He whacked me over the back of the head. "Mr Whitehurst to you, son."

I apologised, walked off and could hear the pair of them laughing in the background.

A few weeks after I signed for Everton in 1987, we had an away game at Oxford United. By this stage Mr Whitehurst was playing for them.

All the talk amongst the Everton players beforehand was how they wanted revenge on Whitehurst because he had badly injured Paul Bracewell's ankle the previous season when Billy was at Newcastle United. I didn't fancy being expected to 'do' Whitehurst, knowing how fearsome he was.

Again, we were on the pitch beforehand and I heard the shout: "Snodin! Come here." I thought: 'Fucking hell, that's Billy.' I walked over and he greeted me by saying: "I'm fucking made up for you, son. Remember all those years ago when we were stood with Billy Bremner and you were 17? You've just signed for the best team in English football. Billy was right, wasn't he?"

I said: "Cheers, Billy" and he whacked me on the head again.

"It's still Mr Whitehurst to you. Now, you go to your team-mates and tell them that if anyone wants to start owt because of what happened with Bracewell, I'll be ready for them and I'll sort it out."

I went into the dressing room and didn't say a word, although there were more shouts about "doing Whitehurst".

Shortly before the kick-off, Kevin Ratcliffe led the players through the narrow tunnel at the Manor Ground onto the pitch. Billy Whitehurst was the third in line and I was right at the back. As the gate opened, I heard him shout: "Snods! Have you fucking warned them all?"

Kev came up to me on the pitch and asked about what Whitehurst had just said. I told our skipper that Billy was expecting our players to go after him and was ready for it. Ratters decided to call off the revenge mission and instructed our players to "leave Whitehurst alone". He was that intimidating.

## HOW MUCH DO YOU EARN, GAZZA?

Soon after I joined Everton, we played Newcastle United when Paul Gascoigne was still only 19. During the match he nutmegged Peter Reid and shouted "nuts" as he did so. Reidy was furious but before he could recover, Gazza knocked the ball past him again on the opposite side. The ball was now heading towards me and as I'd seen and heard all this, I decided to teach the cheeky bugger a lesson. I cleaned him out and he went down squealing.

I said to him: "You cheeky little bastard. Have some respect." After he got up and the game continued, he tried to elbow me off the ball. I wasn't impressed and threatened him: "I'll fucking kill you. Pack it in. Anyway, how much are you on a fucking week?" I should never have said it. I wasn't on megabucks, but he was probably only earning £200 a week at the time.

In December 1988 I played against him again, shortly after he had joined Tottenham in a big-money move. As we waited in the tunnel before kick-off, I was stood across from Gazza and congratulated him on his move. He thanked me by asking: "How much are you fucking on?" He then produced a £20 note that was tucked into his shorts and handed it to me, adding: "You need that more than I do." I was laughing and thought 'fair play, son'. What a comeback.

## A SOAP OPERA

I was called up to the England squad for a World Cup qualifier in Albania in March 1989. Although I'd played against Paul Gascoigne before and seen what a great talent he had, this was the first time I'd experienced his antics at close hand.

Albania had a lot of poverty and the facilities were quite basic, but the people were very friendly and came to watch us train. There had been plenty of heavy rain and after the session finished, Gazza entertained the locals by going in goal and making silly dives. Then he began sliding on his belly across pools of water. The Albanians were loving it and began chanting his name. This must have carried on for about 20 minutes.

Later on, Tony Cottee and I walked past Gazza's hotel room and I could hear the lads inside laughing and joking. Chris Waddle beckoned us in and they asked if we had any chocolate. The FA had supplied us with quite a few bars so I went back to my room and brought them back. We handed them over and Gazza started chopping them into little squares. He then threw the squares out of the window – there must have been 50 Albanian kids at ground level, fighting for this chocolate.

We quickly ran out of supplies, at which point Gazza demanded soap from all our bathrooms. He repeated the trick of chopping it into squares and threw them out of the window. You could see the kids fighting over it before putting it in their mouths. When they realised what they were eating, they went from idolising Gazza to chanting "bastard, bastard".

## GAZZA AND THE GORILLA

Another great Gazza story involving a gorilla and a ham sandwich was told to me by John Moncur, the former Tottenham Hotspur, Swindon Town and West Ham midfielder.

Gazza and his family went to London Zoo with Moncur and his little 'un. After a look at the animals, they opened their picnics for a spot of lunch. The food was spread out on the grass near to the gorilla enclosure.

All through the meal, the gorilla stared at them. Gazza

remarked: "It's probably hungry – give it a sandwich." His then wife, Sheryl, told him to stop being ridiculous but Gazza was insistent. When Sheryl wasn't looking, he quietly asked Moncur if there was anything left in their hamper. There was a ham sandwich going spare, which was placed to the side, out of view. When the opportunity arose, Gazza picked up the butty and threw it into the gorilla enclosure.

The gorilla raced after the sandwich, devoured it and then reared up on its legs, roaring and beating its chest. Gazza was falling about laughing.

Moncur asked: "It's going mental – what have you done?"

"I put a full jar of mustard on the sandwich."

The gorilla's mouth must have been on fire.

## CHAMPIONSHIP

The Everton team of 1986/87 was special with so many players who were comfortable on the ball. Anyone who was half decent could easily fit in. I felt they could have signed anybody.

I don't think I contributed at all to the championship win after I joined in the January. Some people might think I played okay, but I didn't feel part of it. I felt good that we'd won the league but, on reflection, it didn't have much to do with me. My main contribution was turning down Liverpool. It gave the blue half of Merseyside a buzz. Having said all that, nobody can take away my championship medal.

There's no TV footage from that time that I can watch which might remind me of what I might have contributed, apart from the goal at Bradford – which was in the FA Cup.

I played in the game at Norwich where we clinched it. I remember Evertonians being everywhere around the ground. Pat van den Hauwe scored in the first minute and Reidy and I were the first to get to him. When the final whistle went, it was an absolutely fantastic moment.

## SLOSHED AND SHREDDED

Neil Pointon and I used to get loads of stick about our clothes. Mine were bad but not on the scale of Pointon. His gear was horrendous. Before the Norwich game I bought a nice pair of shoes and a lovely suit, shirt and tie. In the dressing room, the lads were saying: "Jesus Christ: Spent a few quid, eh Snods?" They were feeling the material and seemed very impressed.

On the trip back Joanne was due to pick me up at Burtonwood services on the M62 before taking me back to Yorkshire.

There was champagne in the dressing room afterwards and it was the first time I'd drunk it. Drinks were flowing and we set off on the long journey home. It was absolutely buzzing, there was a sing-song on the microphone...the journey was absolutely fantastic. I remember getting as far as Knutsford and I fell asleep.

The next thing I remember was someone shouting: "Snods, get your gear – we're at Burtonwood." I stood up and the sleeves on my jacket came off – the lads had shredded my suit, they'd cut my belt, all down my trousers, my tie, my shirt...I looked like Robinson Crusoe.

The bus doors opened and Joanne wound down her car window. Howard Kendall warned her "wait until you see him". I got to the top of the stairs and my trousers were around my ankles while everything else was cut up. She looked horrified and I mouthed "wankers" at her. All the lads were banging on the windows, in hysterics.

## DOWN UNDER AND ALMOST OUT

After the championship had been won, we went on tour to Australia and New Zealand before finishing with a holiday in Hawaii.

The plane journey got out of hand. We were going on a 24-hour flight and started drinking as soon as the coach left Bellefield. On the plane we were all pissed out of our heads. Our behaviour wasn't great. Pat van den Hauwe caused a bit of a commotion with the stewardesses – I don't know what he was saying, but I can imagine. They should have been wearing trainers because of the number of times they were up and down the aisles, serving us drinks.

Looking back, I think about the other people on the plane, the children, the parents, and what they must have thought of us. We were boisterous, out of order and they probably thought we were dick heads.

The captain of the flight came over the tannoy and told the Everton players to calm down. From that point we were only allowed one drink per person.

We stopped at Los Angeles to refuel. The pilot must have alerted the police because when we disembarked, we saw three or four policemen carrying guns. One fella told the Everton party to follow him. We were taken into a room and told we weren't going any further because we had behaved disgracefully. The plan was to put us on a plane and fly us back to England. It was quite scary. We were representing the club and we were out of order.

We all understood the seriousness of the situation when we heard this. They asked us who was in charge and Adrian Heath pointed to Howard, who was coming towards us. The gaffer was drunk and in a dishevelled state with stains on his shirt caused by Kevin Sheedy throwing red wine over him after an argument. One of the policemen said in disbelief: "That guy is in charge of you?" We started laughing but the officer didn't. "What are you guys laughing at? This is a serious matter," he warned us.

There was a hush and Howard sobered up instantly. He listened to what the officer had to say and gave us all a lecture. He then asked if there were any questions and Adrian Heath lifted his arm. He pointed to Neil Pointon's frizzy hair and asked: "I'd just like to know, where did he get that hat from?" We all started chuckling but the officer wasn't amused. Howard told Adrian to behave himself and stop being stupid, before asking if anybody had "any serious questions". Adrian's arm went up again.

"Where did he get that fucking hat from?"

This time none of us laughed and the officer said, sternly: "I

**Youth team:** Front, third right, with Donny's youngsters. Manager Lawrie Sheffield is back left, with physio Alan McIvor front right

**Signing on:** Penning my first pro contract, flanked by Doncaster Rovers' secretary Roger Read (left) and the boss, Billy Bremner

**Brothers grin:** Glynn (right) and a young child (me) pose for a pre-season photo at Belle Vue, circa 1980

**Main men:** On the first-team photo (front, fourth left), circa 1980

**Early learning:** Cleaning boots with David Harle (above left); my first booking with the youth team against Barnsley (above); dressed as a court jester at a fancy dress 'do', again with Harley (left)

**Hat-trick:** Scoring from the spot in the 7-5 victory over Reading in 1982 – the only treble of my career

**Big influences:** Glynn and I with Billy Bremner and our dad at Belle Vue

**All smiles:** From left: Billy, me, Glynn, Steve Lister and Harley take part in a silly photo stunt (above left), while we celebrate the 1-0 defeat of First Division QPR in the FA Cup, January 1985 (above)

MIMMS, WILKINSON, RIDENT, PICKERING, SEAMAN, CRANSON, BUTTERWORTH, DONOVA, ADAMS

MYSELF, COTTEE, ALLAN, PARKER, BARKER, WALTERS, THOMAS.

**England U21s:** Above – My scrapbook reminder of the England line-up that faced Romania in 1985, and (below) in action against Turkey the previous year

**England:** Training with the full squad in early 1989 with Gazza (above), while my Everton team-mate Tony Cottee watches on

**Leeds man:** The 1986/87 team pic, with me in my favourite kit front, third left. Ian Baird (middle row, first right), John Stiles (front, first left) and John Sheridan (front, first right) are also included

**Signing on:** (Left) With Everton secretary Jim Greenwood and boss Howard Kendall after completing my move, and (above) the centre of attention, January 1987

**Early impact:** Heading my first Everton goal, which proved to be the winner at Bradford in the FA Cup (above); celebrating with Gary Stevens and Paul Wilkinson (left)

**Champions:** (Below) Saluting the fans with (left to right) Bobby Mimms, Neville Southall and Adrian Heath on our lap of honour, May 1987

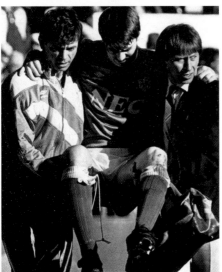

**The life of a footballer:**
Clockwise from top left –
A word with my
opposite number during
our 6-1 mauling by Real
Madrid, August 1987;
celebrating my first
league goal for Everton,
at Newcastle; making it
5-0 in the fourth game
of the 1988 FA Cup
marathon, at Sheffield
Wednesday; the start of
my injury nightmare,
being carried off after
pulling up, again against
Wednesday, March 1989

**Wembley visit:** At the back of the Everton bench during the first half of the 1989 Simod Cup final – Philly Morgan yet to join us

**Ready:** (Above) Warming up ahead of my comeback against Coventry, 1992; Jimmy Martin, Howard Kendall and Colin Harvey watch from the Everton dugout (above right)

**Old rival:** Having my work cut out against John Barnes in the 1993 Anfield derby

don't find you amusing." The guns weren't pointing at us but they were out and the gaffer gave Adrian another bollocking.

We went on to New Zealand and Australia and no more drinks were served.

## HOWARD LEAVES

I was gutted when Howard left to manage Athletic Bilbao in June 1987. I signed a four-year contract in the January and I expected him to be there for the duration. Everton were a successful team and I thought it would go on and on. I could understand why he went, especially with the ban on English clubs competing in Europe, but it was a massive blow to the players and all Evertonians.

## EVERTON ARE LEFT BEHIND

I didn't think we needed to bring anybody in following the championship win. There weren't many players who could have improved that squad. We could have possibly done with another striker but Tony Cottee did arrive in 1988. If we'd have kept the team together and Howard Kendall stayed, we could have gone on and on. I firmly believe that.

The players who came in later on, the likes of Peter Beagrie, Pat Nevin, Stuart McCall and Neil McDonald, were good but they weren't better than what we had before. McCall wasn't better than Peter Reid or Paul Bracewell in their prime. Pat Nevin wasn't as good as Kevin Sheedy or Trevor Steven. That's not a criticism, just a reflection of how talented the established players were. If we were going to bring players in, it should have been the likes of John Barnes and Peter Beardsley, who Liverpool signed in 1987.

After a while you could tell we weren't going to be challenging for top honours. We were always capable of beating the top teams but we were also more vulnerable than had been the case previously.

## MEETING EUSEBIO

We played in a pre-season tournament in La Coruna, Spain, in the summer of 1987 involving ourselves, Sporting Gijon, Benfica and Deportivo La Coruna. I wore the number 10 shirt in the game against Benfica. Afterwards Colin Harvey, who stepped up from first-team coach as Howard's replacement, told me I had to present my top to someone from the Portuguese club.

I showered, changed and headed to the room where I had been directed. There were quite a few photographers inside when I walked in. I discovered the man waiting for me was the great Eusebio, who shook my hand. Colin must have known but he kept it from me as a surprise. I was very lucky I was wearing 10 that night, although I'm sure that Everton top is at the bottom of his wardrobe.

## REAL MADRID HUMILIATION

We played Real Madrid in the Bernabeu in a Super Cup competition shortly after the start of the 1987/88 season. It was a great occasion; the only problem was we didn't have a team. Neville Southall wasn't fit, Adrian Heath didn't go...there were loads of first-team players who weren't involved. We had a really weakened side out. Kevin Sheedy played, but he had only just come back from a calf injury.

Howard Kendall brought his Athletic Bilbao players, club president and directors to the game because he wanted to show them the English champions.

We lost 6-1 and it could have been 26. They were awesome. Sheedy had only done one training session and was in centre-midfield with me. He told me: "You can be my legs tonight." After 20 minutes we were two down and I was breathing out of my arse. He looked at me and shouted: "Where's my legs?" I replied: "Your legs are gone and so are mine."

Bobby Mimms made some brilliant saves. Adrian listened to the game at home on the radio and he told me the only names you'd hear for minutes on end were Real Madrid players – we couldn't get near the ball.

## DUBAI DESPAIR

In December 1987, Everton played Glasgow Rangers for the Dubai Super Cup, which was effectively a British Championship game. We led 2-0 and were absolutely cruising. Graeme Souness was the Rangers player-manager and brought himself on with about 20 minutes to go. His socks were rolled down and Peter Reid told me to watch myself with him. Souness ran the show – he was different class – and they brought the score back to 2-2.

It went to penalties and I missed the crucial spot-kick. Chris Woods, who was the Rangers' keeper, has been the Everton goalkeeper coach for years and likes to remind me about what happened. I was devastated afterwards.

## SETTLING IN

It took me a long time to settle in. At Leeds I had a manager who built the team around me. Billy Bremner would say that if I played well, Leeds played well. At Everton I was just a number because all the other players were just as good as me, if not better. I wouldn't say I was in awe of my team-mates but it took about 15 months to get the best out of me. I don't think I started doing myself justice until I moved to centre-half and then right-back. As the years went by, I became a lot more confident and thought: 'Of course I deserve to be here, I'm a decent player.'

## PLUG AND BERNARD MANNING

There was a young groundsman at Everton called Jimmy Ryan, who was known to everybody as 'Plug' after the character from the Bash Street Kids. He wore glasses, was quite spotty and was not the most intelligent kid we'd ever met. However, we all loved him and he'd do anything for you.

When Colin Harvey was manager, he had an eye on a youth-team game from his office at Bellefield. Terry Darracott was with him and Colin was appalled to notice the lines were not visible – Jimmy had forgotten to paint them before the game. Colin was fuming and demanded that Terry bring Plug to his office.

Terry found him and explained: "The gaffer wants to see you

and he's not happy – he's got a face on for some reason. When you get up there, he's going to ask you a question. Just say: 'There are no runners from midfield'."

Plug went upstairs and knocked on Colin's door.

"Come in...come here you. Look out of that window – what can't you see?"

"There are no runners from midfield."

"You fucking what?"

"There are no runners from midfield."

At this point Colin burst out laughing and Terry Darracott entered the room, in hysterics from setting Plug up.

For Neil Pointon's stag do we travelled to Bernard Manning's club in Manchester. About 12 of us went, including Plug. Bernard had been on for about an hour when he called up anybody who was celebrating their birthday or about to get married. He said there would be a bottle of champagne for all of them.

There were about eight fellas and 10 girls who went up and we talked Plug into pretending it was his birthday. He protested initially but agreed to go on stage when we mentioned the free champagne that he'd get.

Neil stood out of the way at the back. Plug plonked himself right on Bernard's shoulder. He was clocked immediately. There was a blonde-haired girl stood on the opposite side. Bernard looked at the blonde and said: "I wish I was marrying you." As he was talking to her, he kept glancing at Plug. We were wetting ourselves.

Eventually he spoke to Plug. "It must be your birthday, son, because no fucker is going to marry you."

## A SOLO GOAL CELEBRATION

In January 1988 Everton were involved in an epic FA Cup third-round tie with Sheffield Wednesday that went to three replays. The first match had been drawn 1-1 at Hillsborough and unfortunately I missed a one-on-one after being put clean through on Martin Hodge, the Wednesday goalkeeper. After two further 1-1 draws at Goodison, we had to go back to Hillsborough for the fourth match in what felt like a never-ending saga.

The lads were still having a go at me for missing the chance in the first game, blaming me for not sparing us from the replays. All the matches had been tight and we were expecting more of the same in the third replay. However, we absolutely blitzed them in the first half and raced into a 4-0 lead with Graeme Sharp scoring a hat-trick and Adrian Heath getting the other. Shortly before half-time I was sent clean though and slotted past Hodge for the fifth goal. As a former Leeds player, I had been getting plenty of stick from the home support so I ran to their Kop and milked the moment for all it was worth. I was expecting my team-mates to follow but turned round to find they were all standing on the halfway line. I felt like a right dick. There were disgruntled moans along the lines of: "If it wasn't for you, we wouldn't be here now."

## AN INTRODUCTION TO PSYCHO PAT

The day before Doncaster played at Goodison in the FA Cup in 1985, Billy Bremner went through the Everton team with us. When he got to Pat van den Hauwe, who had not long joined the club, he said: "Great defender; gets forward but he's a headcase who easily gets upset and likes to fight." He looked straight at me and sternly added: "Don't get involved."

Early in the game we had to defend a corner and Pat stood close to me at the near post. He tugged at my shirt and I pushed him off. He responded by giving me the van den Hauwe stare so I called him a "fucking idiot" and told him to "fuck off". He didn't like this and butted me right above the eye line. I reacted angrily and the referee jumped in to calm it all down. I looked towards the dugout and Billy was screaming: "Keep your head."

I got on fine with Pat when I joined Everton. He lived in Ainsdale and couldn't drive so whoever was driving out of myself, Neil Pointon, Kevin Sheedy or Ian Wilson would pick Pat up. He was decent with us as a collective but otherwise he could be withdrawn or a bit strange.

Pat kept himself to himself generally. He might train on a

Monday and then you wouldn't see him again until Friday as he went missing for two or three days. If he'd been on a bender, he wouldn't tell you where he'd been. He'd be with his own friends rather than one of the Everton lads. You'd never get to the root of what Pat had been doing.

# CHAPTER 5

# HAMSTRUNG

**A move to a new position brought an England call-up but my dreams were shattered by the start of a three-and-a-half year nightmare. I returned older and heavier as a declining Everton memorably avoided relegation, despite the weak management of a sun-worshipping boss**

*"Snodin had a very, very impressive game, and he is at the right age as well. He could be a possibility for me in the future. Snodin has always been a good passer of the ball, because he played in midfield for so long. All he has to do now is learn a little bit more positional sense at right-back"*

**England manager Bobby Robson, December 1988**

## STOPPED IN MY TRACKS

AFTER his first season in charge at Everton, Colin Harvey was looking to bring in some new players and one of them was Stuart McCall from Bradford City. I appeared to be on my way out because the club had agreed a fee for my transfer to Sheffield Wednesday.

I didn't want to go back to Yorkshire because I'd not played to my potential at Everton. Colin said: "The decision's yours." I responded: "I don't feel I've done myself justice."

Stuart was renowned for being Bradford's best player from a young age and I was Donny's best player. When it came to Leeds v Bradford a few years later, there was always a big build up that it was me versus Stuart McCall. I can't recall one occasion when Stuart got the better of me, I always seemed to dominate him.

I told Colin that I must have played him on a dozen occasions and had never come off second best. I said: "I hope you don't mind but I'm not going to Sheffield Wednesday – I'm going to stay and battle for my place." Colin replied: "No problem, I love to hear that."

In the summer of 1988, Colin also signed Tony Cottee for a British transfer record fee, plus Pat Nevin and Neil McDonald. Kevin Ratcliffe was injured that pre-season and I played centre-back in a practice match against Cottee. I was comfortable there, did well and started the season in that position.

The first game of the season was against Newcastle and they had John Robertson and Mirandinha up front. Cottee scored a hat-trick and received all the plaudits, but I also played well. Mirandinha was quick and at one stage there was a straight race between him and me; I got to the ball comfortably and back-heeled it to Dave Watson.

Where I struggled was in the air. We played against Millwall, Luton Town and Wimbledon and lost all three. Ratcliffe was fit again and Colin explained he would return at centre-back – but then asked if I'd ever played right-back. McDonald had been signed for that position but struggled. I hadn't played there before but Colin told me: "Get ready, you're playing tomorrow."

I was up against Rodney Wallace, who was super fast and I was caught out for the first goal, but we came back to win 4-1 and I played really well. Within two months Colin was telling the England manager, Bobby Robson, that I was the best right-back in the country.

I still saw myself as a midfield player and, initially, to be moved to right-back was a disappointment. I always wanted to get back to midfield but I became a fans' favourite and I did enjoy playing there. Only on one or two occasions was I taken to the cleaners – John Barnes did it once at Anfield.

I was chosen for the England squad for a friendly in Greece in February 1989 and went to Albania for a World Cup qualifier a month later. Although I didn't make the bench, it was great to be there. I believe Bobby Robson told Peter Reid that he was going to play me in the return game at Wembley a few weeks later.

In between those two matches Everton faced Sheffield Wednesday at Goodison on March 11. During the game Kevin Ratcliffe knocked a long ball into the corner and I set off after it. I thought it was going out of play so I hesitated but the ball held up slightly and I set off again. As I did so, I felt searing pain. I'd experienced hamstring pulls before but this felt so different.

I couldn't even walk but I refused to get on a stretcher. Graham Smith, who was a youth-team coach, was one of the people who carried me around the pitch. It was the beginning of a nightmare.

A hamstring injury usually takes four to six weeks to clear up but I was getting to a certain point in my rehabilitation and breaking down. I thought there was more to it then. As soon as I was attempting three-quarter pace, it would go.

I went to see the British Olympic surgeon in London and he operated. It didn't work. I was in pain sitting on a settee and driving my car – I had to drive with my right cheek off the seat because I was in agony. I was told that the aftermath of the surgery was causing the pain, but I knew there was something still wrong in there.

We went down to London to see the surgeon again, keeping my right cheek off the seat. We were in his room for five minutes. His advice was to sit on an inflatable rubber ring to stop the pain. That was it. I looked at Everton's physio, Les Helm, in disbelief.

We went to Middlesbrough for another opinion and the guy we saw thought the source of the problem was a sciatic nerve in my back. He operated and that didn't work. I had three operations and was still no closer to a solution.

I was due to travel to Harvard University in America where my team-mate Paul Bracewell received treatment for his ankle injury. The plan was for them to operate and I was going to do all my rehabilitation over there.

Beforehand I underwent a special scan at the Royal Liverpool Hospital to take over to Harvard and the professor in Liverpool identified the problem – I'd broken the bone which was attached to my hamstring. Every time I attempted to run above half pace, it would tear my hamstring. He told me over the phone they'd found the problem and my first reaction was to say: "No more surgery, please. Let me go over to America."

I went to see the professor that evening and he told me they could operate the following day. He also guaranteed that he wasn't raising my hopes prematurely – this was the cause of all the grief.

I still felt like chucking it in when I got to the hospital. I told the professor: "I'm not doing it, I'm not having surgery over here again." I'd set my mind on going over to America where I believed the best surgeons and rehabilitation centres were based. My head had gone but as soon as I saw the X-ray I realised that he was right.

It took me a long time to go through the rehabilitation because my hamstring had withered so much – it was only at 30% of the strength of the other one.

To be out for two seasons, and not be right for three-and-a-half years, was horrendous. People were saying "it's only a hamstring", but I knew it wasn't that simple. I was in too much pain but nobody could get to the bottom of it. It was so frustrating: I was playing great football, I'd got into the England squad and I believe I could have played a good few times for my country.

While I was injured, I put on a lot of weight, maybe a stone-and-a-half to two stone, and I'd go out drinking because I couldn't see an end to it. I didn't look after myself as well as I should have done but I'd gone through a lot and missed loads of games. I was at the peak of my career at the time and to miss two seasons was a massive blow.

I eventually came back and was made substitute for a league game against Coventry in October 1992. From about 60 minutes, I was nagging Howard Kendall (who was now in his second spell in charge), saying: "Get me on." He replied: "All in good time."

It got to the last 10 minutes and I was annoyed with him because I was desperate to get on. I'd been for a couple of warm ups and the fans had responded. With two minutes to go, he told me to get ready. When I took my tracksuit top off, the whole ground stood up and it brought a tear to my eye. It was a great experience. I don't think I even touched the ball before the referee blew for full-time but that didn't matter. I was back.

What I went through was horrible, but that's life. It was frustrating to watch Everton play, especially in the big games. I remember watching the 4-4 FA Cup replay with Liverpool in February 1991 with my dad, wishing I was out there playing.

While it was all going on I would still visit the dressing room to encourage the boys, and I would be straight in at full-time. I still felt part of it while desperately wanting to be in my kit rather than a suit.

I wasn't as fast when I came back from the injury and I never got to the peak of my fitness again. Looking at pictures from before and after, you can tell the difference in my face.

We were struggling when I returned – we weren't a good side. Good players had left and their replacements weren't up to the same standard.

## HILLSBOROUGH

Although I was injured, I travelled to the FA Cup semi-final between Everton and Norwich City on April 15 1989. It was a great occasion and although Norwich were higher than us in Division One, we were confident that we could beat them. Three-quarters of the ground seemed to be taken up by Evertonians.

I watched the game from the stand. After a while I noticed a message on the scoreboard stating that there had been a delay in the other semi-final between Liverpool and Nottingham Forest at Hillsborough. However, nobody knew exactly what had happened.

Pat Nevin scored early on to put us 1-0 up. Nothing much was said at half-time – it was all about keeping our shape and maintaining the lead. We held out to win 1-0 and everybody was rejoicing. When we got into the dressing room, Colin Harvey told us what had happened at Hillsborough, where 96 Liverpool supporters had been crushed to death. The room fell silent.

On the Saturday after the disaster, I was asked to represent the club as a chain of scarves was formed between Goodison Park and Anfield. It became known as the 'Chain of Hope'.

I went to Anfield with Liverpool's Peter Beardsley and Barry Devonside, whose son, Chris, had died in the disaster.

It was a great privilege to tie that final scarf – it meant a lot to me but I wish I hadn't needed to go. It was very emotional to climb the steps of the Kop and see all the wreaths and all the scarves – from Liverpool fans, Evertonians and fans in general. I purposely wore a red tie. That day demonstrated to me the unity that exists in Liverpool. Whether you were red or blue was immaterial.

## AN UNEXPECTED GUEST ON THE WEMBLEY BENCH

I got to know a lad called Philly Morgan who would travel to all the Everton games, often with tickets I'd given to him. He lived for the club and was quite a character. Although he had free tickets, he enjoyed the buzz of blagging his way into places. He loved it if he could make a train journey and avoid paying. For most away games, the complimentary tickets I'd given him would be passed on to his pals and he'd find a way of getting in for free.

Shortly after I first suffered my hamstring injury, we played Nottingham Forest in the final of the Simod Cup at Wembley in April 1989. I watched the game from the bench with Neil Pointon. At half-time I decided to stay where I was, rather than make the long walk to the dressing room and back. I was chatting away with Neil when I saw Philly. He was wearing a suit and tie with a pass hanging from his neck while talking to a steward.

Philly approached and told us it had been a "piece of piss" to reach us because he'd claimed to be an Everton official. He also revealed that he intended to sit with us on the bench for the second half. We thought this was a ridiculous idea but he insisted. I told him Colin Harvey would go berserk, but that didn't deter him.

Colin, Terry Darracott and Mike Lyons were sat on the first row. The second row was the substitutes and then it was the likes of Pointon and me who weren't involved, plus our new companion. Colin didn't notice Philly and I pleaded with him not to draw attention to himself. He'd had a few to drink so I was quite worried.

The Forest staff emerged, among them Brian Clough, the manager, plus Archie Gemmill and Liam O'Kane, who were coaches. Clough, who'd also had a drink, decided to sit on the third row, directly opposite us. Within seconds Philly, quite loudly, greeted him and Clough responded by saying: "Hello, young man."

Early in the second half, Gemmill and O'Kane were trying to catch the attention of Stuart Pearce, who was playing left-back on our side of the pitch. They must have shouted him five times at the top of their voices, without success. Philly lost patience, stood up and shouted: "Fucking shut up, you pair of seals."

Colin and Terry turned around and I shrugged my shoulders at them. Brian Clough then piped up.

"Hey, young man. I was done a few months ago for swearing on the bench. Come here."

Philly walked over to the Forest bench and sat next to Clough, who put his arm round him. They chatted away for the next five or 10 minutes. When Philly came back to our side, he revealed he'd told Cloughie about his daughter's dance group and asked for a signed shirt so they could raise some money.

At the end of the game, which Forest won 4-3 after extra-time, Philly waited 10 minutes before knocking on their dressing room door. Clough let him in and provided the signed shirt. That was Philly Morgan to a tee.

## THE WRATH OF HARVEY

When we reported back for pre-season training in 1989, I upset Colin Harvey by weighing more than I should have done.

Injured players were expected to return early but I arrived on the same day as the rest of the lads.

As soon as I walked in, Terry Darracott, the assistant manager, said: "Why weren't you back early? The gaffer is fuming with you." All the lads were calling me "squirrel" because I had puffy jowls, asking: "Where have you been all summer? Look, he's storing his nuts for winter." I could see Colin and I was thinking, 'Boys, please: Do not give him any ammunition.'

After the first session, we were due to have a short break before some running. I was waiting for my new sponsors, Asics, to deliver some trainers. It was a boiling hot day and everyone was taking drinks on board. Then I heard Colin shout: "Get your shirt tucked in." There were about 12 or 13 of us with our shirts out so we all looked around. I asked: "Who?" and he replied: "Fucking you." The lads were pissing themselves.

I did as I was told, and then he bawled: "Where's your trainers?"

"They've not arrived yet from Asics."

"I'll get you some."

I take a size 6, but he came marching back with a pair of size 10s. "Get them on," he roared. I started laughing.

"What are you fucking laughing at?"

"I can't wear them – I'll look like Coco the clown."

"Just fucking get them on."

I tried to protest when I was tying them up, but Colin wasn't in the mood for a debate. "Just fucking run in them."

The lads were howling as I ran in these canoes but it was my own fault – I should have been in earlier.

After two days of training, Colin was still not talking to me. We had practice games organised against Oldham at Bellefield for the first team and reserves. I was a sub for the first-team game. Joe Royle was Oldham manager and was surprised I wasn't starting. I told him the situation and he said: "Don't worry, Colin loves you to death. He wishes he had 11 of you in the team. Get your head down, get your weight off and you'll start the season, no problem."

Colin put me on after about 60 minutes. It was roasting. Unfortunately, I played a short backpass and Roger Palmer collided with Neville Southall as they both tried to collect it. Colin went potty.

At the end of the game we walked towards a big tub of ice-cold Gatorade. Colin interrupted: "What are you fucking doing? Put it down."

"You begrudge me a drink of orange?"

"I fucking do. Put it down – you're going on in the other game."

Mike Lyons was the reserve-team manager and I had to tell him that Colin insisted I play immediately. He said: "No problem, I'll wait for the ball to go out of play and I'll make a change." I stood alongside Lyons and the ball stayed in play for over a minute. There was a shout from the manager's office, which overlooked the pitch.

"Stop the game. Lyonsey, get him on that field now." On I

went. For the next two weeks he stayed on my case but it was only because he cared. He wanted me fit and in the team.

## SOUR GRAPES

Howard Kendall would let us have a laugh and a drink after any match, no matter what the result. Colin Harvey was stricter. There was fruit and pasta on the bus with no alcohol, just orange juice. He would sit at the front and if we'd been beaten, he wouldn't talk to anybody. He would watch a video and as soon as one finished, he'd put another on. We would be playing cards but nobody dared to laugh.

On one away journey back from London, Jimmy Martin, who at the time was the coach driver and is now the kit manager, approached us and announced: "That's it – I'm not doing this job anymore."

"Why?"

"Fucking Colin. He knows I love him but he's out of order. I think this job is getting to him. He's just had a go at me about the grapes. He'd ordered seedless and I got some with seeds. I've just had a massive bollocking."

I've got great respect for Colin as he's a top fella, but he was a coach rather than a manager. I don't think man-management was his forte. On the training field he was brilliant, but he found it difficult to have a one-to-one meeting in his office with a player. I wish we could have done better under him because he absolutely loved the club.

## HOWARD SECOND TIME AROUND

I was delighted when Howard Kendall returned in November 1990, following Colin Harvey's sacking. I had so much respect for him as a person and as a manager.

Unfortunately I was in the middle of my bad injury. Not long after I came back, in autumn 1992, we beat Nottingham Forest at the City Ground and Howard said afterwards that having me back was like signing a new £1m player. Hearing things like that made you desperate to play for the man.

Initially I couldn't play two games within a week because I would be in agony for two or three days immediately after a match. In March 1993 I wanted to play at Stamford Bridge on the Wednesday after a Sunday game at Coventry City. I wasn't as sore as usual, but Howard didn't include me. I was furious but he had done it to protect me, long-term.

In his second spell, we were nowhere near as good as 1987 and he was simply trying to make the best of what he had. He was always bubbly around the club and made you feel relaxed – a terrific man-manager. If he hadn't behaved in that way, maybe we would have been relegated.

He left in December 1993, just after we'd beaten Southampton 1-0 at Goodison. Two or three of us heard the news on radio when we were driving back to Southport. Howard had wanted to sign Dion Dublin from Manchester United but the board wouldn't sanction the move. There had been no sign of any issues after the game. I was bitterly disappointed – everybody was. We all wanted to play for him. It was a total shock. On the following Monday when we were back in training, nobody could believe it. You learn that you just have to accept such happenings in football because managers come and go.

## EGGING MARK WARD ON TO CHIP NEVILLE SOUTHALL
Soon after I signed for Everton, Kevin Sheedy tried to get me to chip Neville Southall during shooting practice but Nev had already warned me not to try it. All goalkeepers hate being chipped. Any Everton player who defied his wishes would face fearful consequences. I wasn't stupid enough to wind him up.

When Mark Ward joined in 1991 I quickly suggested that he chip Nev. Wardy is a bubbly, fiery scouser and was happy to take on the challenge. When he'd sent the ball over his head, Nev chased after him and gave him a good few digs.

## A DERBY WIN AND LIP FROM BILLY KENNY
In December 1992, shortly after I returned to the team, I started a Monday night derby game against Liverpool at Goodison. John

Barnes played against me and it was a real battle. With about 20 minutes to go they brought Mark Walters on so Howard Kendall took me off because I was knackered.

Peter Beardsley, who was in his second season at Everton after joining us from Liverpool, scored the winning goal in the final 10 minutes. The first person he ran to was me on the bench. My performance received plenty of praise afterwards.

Another Everton player who did well that night was Billy Kenny. Billy was a scally but an entertaining lad. He was full of himself in a funny way, even as a young kid.

During my injury absence in 1990/91 I watched an 'A' team game and went into the dressing room afterwards.

Everton lost and the coach, Jim Barron, was having a go at them. The first team were playing at Goodison later that day and Jim told the goalkeeper, Jamie Speare, to study every aspect of Neville Southall's performance. He wanted the right-back, John Doolan, to watch me when I was fit again. Neil Moore, who later played in the first team on a few occasions, was told to emulate Dave Watson. He reached Billy Kenny and said: "Billy, when you get to Goodison this afternoon, you watch Mike Milligan."

Billy, who was about 17, responded: "You what? Mike Milligan ought to have been here this morning watching fucking me."

Billy had so much talent. I don't know if more could have been done to stop him going off the rails. It depends on what kind of character you are. Maybe he didn't have as strict an upbringing as me. It was hard to nail him down and he just did what he wanted.

## EVERTON CAPTAINCY

I captained every club I played for, including Everton. It might not have been a long-term appointment as with Kevin Ratcliffe but to skipper Everton was a great honour.

In February and March 1990 we played Oldham in the fifth round of the FA Cup in a tie that lasted three games. We eventually lost the second replay on Boundary Park's plastic pitch on a day I was skipper. Colin Harvey was devastated and I was fuming. As I looked around the dressing room afterwards, there were one or two who didn't appear that bothered by the result. I threw my boots against the wall in anger and ranted about us needing to have a look at ourselves. I went crazy for a minute. Colin came up to me afterwards and said: "I wish I had another 10 players like you, lad. We'd have waltzed through this cup tie." He was talking about my attitude rather than my ability. I wasn't the most skilful but I possessed an immense will to win.

It was a tradition of pre-season training to have a five-a-side competition. Every year I would captain a team and they would be known as 'Snodin's Snarlers'. If I disagreed with any refereeing decisions, I would swear and curse to whoever was in charge – Colin Harvey, Terry Darracott or Mike Lyons.

In January 1994 we played Manchester United two days after the death of Sir Matt Busby, their legendary former manager. There was only one empty seat in Old Trafford that day and it was his. Steve Bruce led United out and I led Everton, with a lone bagpiper in front of us. From the moment we took our places in the tunnel, it was so eerie. You could have heard the proverbial pin drop. The whole ground was hushed. When we received the nod to walk out, the bagpiper started playing. Apart from his tune, there was absolute silence and it felt like it lasted for about 10 minutes. It was an experience I'll never forget and I was proud to be Everton captain that day.

## MW

Mike Walker had done well at Norwich, they'd finished third in the Premier League and beaten Bayern Munich in the UEFA Cup, but on his first day as Everton manager in January 1994 I thought, 'I'm not sure about you.'

Bellefield had been pretty much unchanged since the 1960s. He came along and got the groundsman to paint 'MW' on the closest parking space to the entrance. Every manager had that space anyway, but he wanted to make a show of it. He never used to arrive until 10-10.15am whereas every other manager would be in by about 8.30.

The day after his initials had been painted on, Mark Ward arrived before the manager and drove right into the space. We were all laughing about it when Walker arrived.

"Whose car is in my space?"

Wardy said: "What? What's your space?"

"I had the groundsman paint 'MW' on the one in front of the entrance."

"I'm sorry gaffer. I thought it was 'MW' for Mark Ward."

He fined him half-a-week's wages because he couldn't see the joke.

You would always respect your manager but it wasn't long before I began to doubt him. I didn't think his training sessions were very good – seasoned professionals were being spoken to as though they were 14-year-old kids. When he had 'MW' painted on the parking space, I thought 'not for me'. It was about a month or six weeks after he arrived when I completely lost faith.

I'd known him to go into the Continental nightclub in Liverpool with 'MW' on his tracksuit top. He was distinctive enough with the shock of white hair. That just summed him up.

At the end of the season we went to Magaluf for a holiday, as was the tradition. We would occupy the beach bar, have a drink, a laugh and a sing-song. There was a tab going and Dave Watson and I looked after the money. Kevin Sheedy was at Blackpool at the time and their players were at the resort too.

On one particular day we were already at the bar when Mike Walker came down and cheerily shouted: "Morning, boys."

I responded: "Hi gaffer, how are you? Do you want a drink?"

"No, no, I'm going to get a bit of sun."

He loved the sun. He went over to the beach, stood up, took his t-shirt and shorts off and revealed the skimpiest pair of red trunks you've ever seen in your life. He's stood up, oiling himself, and we were all going: "Fucking look at him. Fucking idiot."

About half-an-hour later, I happened to say: "Gaffer, do you want a drink now?" He put his hands behind his head, stretched as high as he could and eventually replied: "Go on then, Snowy. I'll have a bottle of Bud." This carried on every time we asked.

After a while the lads started to disperse. It ended up with Dave Watson, Kev Sheedy and myself left. It got to about 5pm and we asked for the bill (we had been there since 10am). We were shocked by the size of it and started emptying our pockets. We were still short. Sheeds had only been with us for two hours and he was emptying his pockets. I shouted at Walker, who was still on his sunbed. "Gaffer, have you got any money?"

"Yes, Snowy."

"We need help with the tab."

"I've only had four beers."

He came walking over with the exact money. I turned to Dave and said: "He's having a fucking laugh, isn't he?" We eventually mustered enough money to pay the bill but he would only contribute for his four beers.

Next day he came down and all the talk had been about him being a tight bastard. I was losing my rag and telling people not to offer him a drink. But somebody did ask him and it carried on from there.

However, he'd brought down a bum bag and left it on a table close to us. I pointed this out to Dave and told him I was going to take Walker's money. We continued asking him if he wanted drinks until 3pm when we asked for the bill. We took his money, paid the bill and gave them a big tip too. Then we told Walker we were moving on to the next bar.

"Snowy, Waggy, I'll get a bit more sun and then I'll join you."

"Don't worry, we've sorted the bill out."

"That's great, thanks lads."

We hadn't been in the new bar long when he came marching up, pointing the finger at me. "You little twat," he said.

"What?"

"I've just gone in my bag and there's not a penny in there."

"Yes, and you gave the waiter a tip."

He went berserk and asked the lads for money to cover his losses. If it was any other manager he would have paid the bill and got on with it. Not him. That was Mike Walker all over. You couldn't really take him seriously. He was a weak character.

## WIMBLEDON – MY FAVOURITE GAME

On the final day of the 1993/94 season, we needed to beat Wimbledon to have a chance of staying up. We weren't a good side but we shouldn't have been facing relegation. And of all the teams to play...

I arrived at Goodison at 1.30pm and there were loads of fans who wanted to be inside early. There were usually 300 in there at that time; on this occasion it was about 6,000. The Park End was a building site as it was being redeveloped, but the atmosphere was still fantastic.

As 3pm approached, the bell went and we walked down the tunnel. Vinnie Jones, who was in the Wimbledon team, was bawling and shouting: "Come on. Let's send these down today."

The atmosphere was fantastic, the ground was absolutely rocking. We had some decent characters who loved a battle; Barry Horne, myself, Dave Watson, Neville Southall. There was apprehension and nervousness but we were really up for it; you could sense it in the dressing room – perhaps not from Mike Walker, but from the players. I can remember the last thing he said: "Keep it tight, don't give anything away."

The game starts and they're kicking towards the Gwladys Street. They get a corner after four minutes, which Anders Limpar, the smallest fella on the pitch, jumps up and hand-balls. We're all thinking: 'Fucking hell, Anders, what are you doing mate?' They score from the penalty but the crowd are still baying for it. Then we fell 2-0 down after 20 minutes because of a Gary Ablett own goal. I honestly thought there was no way back – we were playing Wimbledon, we were two goals down and the crowd were now silent.

Then Anders got in the Wimbledon box and was scythed

down...fucking hell, what a dive that was. The referee pointed to the spot. No-one appeared to fancy it but Graham Stuart said "give me the ball" and sent Hans Segers the wrong way.

We were back in it at 2-1 and the crowd were right up for it. There were people up in the trees in Stanley Park, looking out over Goodison. It was something else.

There was nothing from Walker at half-time but the players were all pumped up. We couldn't wait to get out there. I was banging on the Wimbledon dressing room door on the way out, shouting: "Come on, then. We're ready. Come on."

I took my right-back position in front of the Lower Bullens as we were attacking the Gwladys Street in the second half. There were usually a few lads in wheelchairs at the side of the pitch and I knew all the faces. On this day there were loads of wheelchairs and I didn't recognise many of them. I was laughing to myself about it.

The game re-started. Midway through the second half, Barry Horne hits a screamer that flies into the top corner. The place went berserk and everyone was jumping on Horne's back but I preferred to celebrate with supporters. I was stood on the halfway line, pumping my fist. I turned round to see big Nev's reaction: nothing. I then turned to the Lower Bullens to be greeted by 20 people out of their wheelchairs.

The clock was ticking down and we still needed another goal. I kept asking the ref how long was left. Then Stuart picked the ball up and played it forward to Tony Cottee; it hit his shin and bounces back to Stuart whose shot bobbled 14 times and, somehow, Hans has missed the ball. 3-2 Everton.

Stuart set off on a run to the corner flag, to be chased by eight blue shirts – but not me. I was roaring on the halfway line with my arms outstretched. I turned round to big Nev again: nothing other than a thumbs-up. Then I turned to the Lower Bullens and it was going absolutely crazy. They were all out of their wheelchairs and doing forward rolls and cartwheels. Two of them were on my back, shouting: "Snowy, it's a fucking miracle."

I don't know whether they meant our comeback or their forward rolls.

What a great day. The scenes after the game were something else. As soon as the final whistle went, everybody was running on the pitch. I managed to get down to the tunnel and before I could reach the dressing room, I was dragged into the players' lounge. It was absolutely wild and everyone was going berserk. One of my pals, Ronnie Galvin, gave me a bottle of Bud and I was sat there in my kit, with my socks pulled down and my boots still on. I had four bottles of beer before I went back to the dressing room to have a bath and get changed.

People ask: 'What's the best game you've ever been involved in?' For me, that is. I played in some good matches, such as when we won the championship at Norwich, but to be involved in that match and keep Everton up, the way we did, was special.

I know it's been suggested that it was fixed but if you look at the Wimbledon players, there were a lot of strong characters, like Vinnie Jones and Robbie Earle. Hans Segers should have saved the winning goal but no goalkeeper in the world would have got to Barry Horne's equaliser.

A keeper is in the best position to influence a game but I find it difficult to accept that other players could be involved. They went 2-0 up and had quite a few chances. Why would they do that if they were looking to throw a game? Before the match-fixing story came out, it didn't enter my head that there was anything dodgy about the match. I'm far from convinced that it was fixed. There are only one or two people who know for sure and it's not the lads on the Everton team.

# CHAPTER 6

# RAZOR & SHARP

**After eight years as a blue, I was given a Royle send-off
and headed up the M62 to join an old mate. I didn't receive
a warm welcome from the Oldham crowd, and there was
abuse from a man who terrified Alan Shearer by putting
tights over his head**

*"We've given him a 'free' in recognition of his services.
Ian has done well for us despite a run of injury
problems."*

**Joe Royle, Everton manager, December 1994**

## LEAVING EVERTON

WE played Portsmouth in the League Cup in October 1994 in what turned out to be my final appearance for the club. We had lost the first leg of the second-round tie 3-2 at Goodison a couple of weeks earlier.

In the second leg at Fratton Park, Pompey brought on a quick winger called Paul Hall, who gave me a hard time. We led 1-0 but they scored a late goal to win 4-3 on aggregate. After the match Mike Walker said he couldn't fault the performance and told us he wouldn't be making any changes for the league match to follow at Southampton on the Saturday. When it came to the game there was one player left out – me. I was livid.

After the Southampton match, the players who hadn't taken part were supposed to do some running around the pitch. I refused so he said I'd be fined. On the Monday I went into his office and told him I wasn't going to pay the fine. The following night I played in a reserve game at Derby County, after which I was told the then Sunderland manager, Mick Buxton, wanted to speak to me about a loan move.

It was all organised quickly and I was training with them by the Thursday. Walker tried to convince me that I could play some games, get fit and come back into the Everton team. I knew he was talking shit. He also said that they would forget the fine but within a few days I received a letter from the club, saying I'd been fined two weeks wages.

I was put up in a hotel in Sunderland. There were some good lads at the club who liked a social. They kept coming to the hotel for meals and a drink because the club was picking up my tab. When they received the first bill after a week, Mick asked how many people were staying with me. I came back to Everton six pounds heavier than when I left.

While I was up there, Walker was sacked. The new manager, Joe Royle, wanted me back but I knew he would want to bring in his own players. I was 31, which was no age. I still felt I had a lot to offer but I'd had my time at Everton.

Joe's assistant was Willie Donachie and, in the short time I spent with him, I didn't enjoy his training. Joe was a terrific man-manager but Willie did all the coaching and I found his approach regimental. If there were three five-a-side matches going on, he would stop all three if he was making a point in one of them.

I made a couple of appearances in the reserves and was playing as well as anybody, but I didn't get a chance. There was nothing personal between Joe and I but he wanted his own men.

I'd had eight great years at Everton. There were difficult times, especially when I was injured, but they were eight years I'll never forget. I had the choice of Liverpool or Everton and, in my eyes, choosing Everton was the best decision I've ever made.

## A LONG MEETING WITH SHARPY AND A MOVE TO OLDHAM

When Joe left Oldham to go to Everton, Graeme Sharp replaced him as manager. He called me up and asked if I was interested in joining him so we arranged to meet at an Italian restaurant in Southport, where we both lived. We met at about 6.30pm and football wasn't even mentioned for the first four hours or so. At 11pm I finally asked about the contract and he was ultra relaxed, saying they'd offer whatever I was earning at Everton. That was it. The talks lasted 30 seconds, the drinking session lasted five hours and I had a two-year contract, beginning in January 1995.

As well as Sharpy, I teamed up with Colin Harvey again, who was the assistant manager. It was home from home. I enjoyed it and treated them with the utmost respect.

## SEEING RED ON DEBUT

My Oldham debut was against the team where I had spent six weeks on loan earlier in the season – Sunderland. I didn't enjoy the best of starts.

I was booked early in the game and with about 20 minutes to go I went to tackle their full-back, Martin Scott, following a throw-in. I did lunge in but didn't touch him. He went down as though I'd broken his leg. The referee showed me a second yellow so I was off. I was furious and walked over to Scott to ask: "What are you playing at?" As I trudged off, I shouted to Mick Buxton: "Get a grip of your left-back. He's a fanny."

After the game I saw Scott, who was about to enter the players' lounge. He was wearing a tracksuit and a pair of trainers with no socks. I shouted: "Hey: Lift your tracksuit bottom up – I want to see the mark on your leg." He was reluctant so I grabbed the leg of the tracksuit and pulled it up. There was no mark. His play-acting was a snide thing to do.

## OUT OF THE RUNNING

Training was quite physical, which was strange as Sharpy hated intense work as a player. He gave us a 12-minute run one day after the morning session and told us that if anybody finished behind Jim Cassell, who was chief scout at the time, they'd have to do the run again.

During the exercise, I kept asking how long was left because I hated every second of it. I was aware that Jim was five yards behind me. I was flagging and he was soon on my shoulder. I said to him: "Jim, if you beat me, I'll break your legs. Just stay with me." He promised he would but after another 30 seconds he kicked on. I couldn't stay with him and he beat me by about half-a-lap. The three lads who finished behind him were Paul Gerrard, the goalkeeper, Sean McCarthy, a striker, and myself. I protested and told Sharpy that Jim would have beaten him as well. After five minutes' rest we were brought to the starting line to go again. The players then burst out laughing – they'd set me up. Jim Cassell used to run half-marathons and had fantastic stamina. As a new player, I had no idea.

## THE SHARP EDGE OF RAZOR'S TONGUE

We had a home game on a Saturday and Liverpool weren't due to play until the following day so I invited Neil Ruddock, a great mate of mine, to come and watch.

He was injured so I picked him up from Melwood, Liverpool's

training ground, after he had received treatment. While we were driving along the M62 to Boundary Park, I started telling him about the stick I was getting from the Oldham fans. They didn't want Sharpy to begin with so they weren't keen on me because of the Everton connection. They saw it as jobs for the boys. Razor's reaction was to say "fuck them", but I explained that because the crowds were smaller at Oldham, you could hear all the insults.

When we got to the ground, I gave Razor a match ticket, a ticket to the players' lounge and left him to it. After a minute of the game, the ball went out for a throw-in near the dugouts and I trotted over to take it. As the ball boy passed me the ball, I heard the shout: "Get Snodin off, Sharpy, he's shit!" I thought: 'Jesus Christ, one minute into the game.' I looked up to find my abuser and saw Razor. He was the only one stood up in the Main Stand, pointing at me and repeating: "Get Snodin off, he's shit!" I should have known better than to say something to him. After the game he was laughing his head off in the players' lounge.

## MUSTANG SNODS AND RAZOR

After I got to know Razor, we began to go out on a Saturday night if we'd both played that day. Quite often we'd end up in the Kingsway nightclub in Southport where Gary the DJ was always happy to play our song requests. Once we'd had a few, we both fancied ourselves as singers. On one night we picked up the microphone from the DJ's stand and began belting out 'Mustang Sally'.

The following week the pair of us were stood at the bar when we heard Gary announce: "Right, it's that time of the night, ladies and gentlemen: Snods and Razor with Mustang Sally!" It became a ritual for months. If Ruddock calls me now, he'll say hello by singing the song down the line.

## RUDDOCK BREAKS INTO SHEARER'S BACK GARDEN

Razor told me a great tale involving Alan Shearer, dating from a Blackburn Rovers-Liverpool game at Ewood Park in the mid-1990s.

During the match Ruddock trampled on Shearer, sparking a confrontation between the pair of them, who had been team-mates at Southampton and remained close friends and neighbours. 'Razor' went over to apologise while Shearer was receiving treatment but Al told him to "fuck off". After the game Shearer was due to give Ruddock a lift home to Formby, where they both lived, but in the players' lounge afterwards the great striker still had a face on him.

When they were about to leave, Al got in his car. Razor followed and just as he was about to get in, Shearer drove forward 10 yards before braking. Razor acknowledged the gag, moved forward and the same thing happened. Razor said: "Good one, Al", and walked ahead to catch the car up. On the third occasion Shearer drove off without stopping and flicked Razor the V-sign out of the window. Ruddock had to flag a taxi, which cost him £70.

The following day they spoke over the phone and Razor told him he'd get his revenge. Shearer suggested a game of golf, offering Ruddock the chance to win his £70 back. Al won so as it was double or quits, Razor was now £140 down.

That evening Razor went back to his Missus and kids. Shearer's family was away in Southampton so he was home alone. Ruddock knew Al didn't like being on his own so decided to strike back. He asked his Missus for a pair of her tights, put them over his head and went into Shearer's back garden. He looked through the patio and saw Al on the settee, watching Crimewatch. Razor banged on the window and Shearer jumped up, screaming, while Ruddock scampered back to his house. He sat down when he got there, laughing his head off.

Within seconds the telephone rang and it was a petrified Shearer, telling Razor he'd just seen someone in his garden. Ruddock had to talk him out of ringing the police by saying he'd come round and check to see if there was anyone lurking in the grounds. He took a one iron out of his golf bag and headed over. Razor was ready to strike with the club, effectively looking for himself.

They both went in the garden with Razor acting very bravely while Shearer stood about 10 yards behind. Ruddock shouted: "Come out wherever you are, you bastard. I'll have you." He checked in trees and bushes but, unsurprisingly, didn't find anyone.

Shearer asked Razor if he could stay in his house that night, and Ruddock said it wouldn't be a problem. Al locked up and they went to Razor's where a rattled Shearer sat down and was offered a cup of tea. Ruddock and his Missus were in hysterics in the kitchen. Razor went to take the tea into the front room but had to keep going back because he couldn't maintain a straight face.

Ruddock reassured Al and they watched the rest of Crimewatch. After the programme finished, Razor showed Shearer to his room and left him for half-an-hour. At that point he went back upstairs with the tights over his head again and the one iron in his hand. He banged on Shearer's door and yelled: "They're in my house, Al! They're in my house!" Ruddock then burst into the bedroom to frighten Shearer again. When he saw who it was, Al spat out: "You fucking fat bastard."

## AN EASY APPEARANCE FEE

Before the penultimate game of the 1995/96 season, Graeme Sharp told me to have a rest. All I could think about was my £250 appearance fee. He said he was going to make me substitute but I wanted to start the game. We argued over it but he insisted on making me sub, which I had to accept.

Towards the end of the match I told Sharpy to put me on and mentioned my appearance money. His reaction was to ask: "Do I get a drink out of it?" When I said yes, he agreed to bring me on. As soon as I entered the pitch, the referee blew his whistle for full-time. I shook hands with the players, walked off and Sharpy said: "You fucking owe me." His drink was a bottle of champagne.

## SMOKING A CIGAR

Sharpy was eventually sacked in February 1997 and Neil Warnock replaced him. On his first day, Neil set out a 50-yard pitch for a 13-a-side match. It was freezing. There were tackles flying in and while I was happy to mix it with anybody, I didn't want to get involved in this so I stood on the right wing and didn't move. The game had been going for 20 minutes and I hadn't had a touch. It was ridiculous.

Neil called me over and asked: "What's up?"

I responded: "What's this all about?"

"I just want to see who's got bottle and who's up for a fight. Don't worry, just show a little bit more enthusiasm but I know, when it comes to a match, you'll be wired in." He later asked for my opinion on certain players and generally was good to me. I liked Neil.

We played at Loftus Road towards the end of my time at Oldham when we were heading for relegation. In contrast, QPR were playing really good football. Neil called me in the day before and explained: "I want you to play in what I call the 'cigar position.'" I responded: "Oooh, that'll suit me, no problem. Where's that, sweeper?"

"No, I want you to sit in front of the back four and you'll have a cigar in your mouth. Just intercept anything."

It was baking hot when the game kicked off and QPR were brilliant from the start, passing the ball everywhere at speed. After 20 minutes the sweat was pouring off me, I had never worked so hard. During a break in play, I walked over to the bench and exclaimed: "Gaffer, fucking cigar position? It went out 10 minutes ago." He burst out laughing.

They continued to batter us but we scored in the 33rd minute and held on to win 1-0. Warnock came on the pitch at full-time, walked straight up to me, gave me a kiss and said: "Lovely cigar, wasn't it?" He was a fiery character but great to play for.

## A SEASON BY THE SEASIDE

I was 34 in 1997 and coming towards the end. I was considering an offer from Scarborough when I received a phone call from Micky Adams, who was in charge at Fulham, asking me to come down for a few days so they could take a look at me.

They trained at Epsom, near Gatwick Airport. I got stuck in traffic on the M25 and it took six-and-a-half hours to get there. I didn't need that hassle. Joanne and the kids weren't going to move south for the sake of a year or two, and I didn't want to stay down there for two or three days a week.

Despite this, the training session went well and the following day we played Crystal Palace in a practice match. I strolled it and Micky said: "I've seen enough, you're different class. We'll sign you but we'll give you some fitness tests just to make sure everything is okay. It'll be a doddle for you."

The tests were very stern. That made my mind up as the lads had told me Micky ran them hard every day. I went up to his office and he was ready to write out the contract details. He said: "You were fantastic today but you found that running hard, didn't you?"

I replied: "I found it that hard, Mick, I'm not fucking signing."

"You what?"

"Mick, I can't run like that."

"I like my teams fit."

"That doesn't really bother me, mate, but it took me six-and-a-half hours to get down here and I can't put my Missus through that. I don't want to live down here and I've got the chance of a two-year contract at Scarborough, which is an hour and 15 minutes from my house. I'm going to sign for them."

There was no comparison between the two clubs. At the time, Scarborough were getting 2,000, Fulham 8,000 on a good day, but it was going to make life a lot easier at home to be based in Yorkshire.

## A MAN IN THE KNOW

On one of my first days at Scarborough, I sat next to a little bald midfielder, Ben Worrall, who was 21 at the time. I'd taken a Racing Post or Sporting Life into training and the conversation turned to horse racing. Someone mentioned that Ben's father was good for a few tips. I said to him that I'd be grateful if he passed on any information that his dad had.

A couple of days later Ben told me his dad was going to back a horse running that afternoon at Wincanton. I put a fiver on each-way and it won easily at 7-1. I gave Ben a tenner out of my winnings as I knew he wouldn't be earning big money, and thanked him. He then revealed that his dad was Johnny Worrall – the travelling head man for Nicky Henderson, one of the leading national hunt trainers. I said: "You fucking what? Why didn't you tell me? I'd have had £100 on it, not a poxy fiver." During the season I spent there, I got some great tips from Ben.

I had a good time at Scarborough (who were then in what is now called League Two). We got into the play-offs, but lost 7-2 on aggregate in the semi-finals to Torquay – I was suspended from the second leg because I'd been sent off in the final league game at Chester. I enjoyed the training, I enjoyed the company of the players and I would have happily played for another season. As it was, I didn't stay because a friend in need required my help.

# CHAPTER 7

# THE BOSS

**Winding down my playing career at Scarborough, I received an SOS call to rescue Doncaster from oblivion. I was now a manager with new worries and responsibilities, among them finding 11 fit players to make up a team and dealing with a disruptive foreign import**

*"I've got Doncaster at heart. I arrived here as a 14-year-old and had some great times, winning promotion twice"*

**Ian Snodin, Doncaster Star, August 1998**

## SNODIN THE MANAGER

IN one of my matches for Scarborough, we played Doncaster Rovers in November 1997. They were about to go down with 34 defeats, the most in the history of the Football League. They came out in yellow shirts, brown shorts and yellow socks. I remembered them in red and white and thought: 'They don't even look like a team.' We beat them 4-0.

At one point I was stood on the goalpost at a corner and the Rovers' fans were pleading with me to come back to Donny. They were in a state – the kit didn't look right and the players didn't give a shit. The chairman, Ken Richardson, had tried to burn down the ground in 1995 to claim insurance money and it did seem that this was going to be the end of Donny Rovers. Before the final league match of the 1997/98 season, a mock coffin was carried from the town centre to Belle Vue. The last rites were performed and the Last Post was played. The crowds were down to 750 when previously 3,000 would have been low; nobody would sponsor them; nobody would touch them. They won only four league games that season and finished with a goal difference of minus 83. It was a sham.

A company registered in the Isle of Man, Westferry, bought the club. They didn't know a lot about football but had been asking people in the local community who was required to get the club back up and running.

Ian McMahon, the chief executive who fronted the Westferry consortium, was the first person who spoke to me. I received a phone call from him in the summer of 1998. He explained who he was and asked if I'd be interested in managing Doncaster Rovers. He told me he'd asked around the town who the club needed and the answer tended to be "the Snodin brothers". I'd never met him before.

My only condition was that Ken Richardson wasn't involved. I told Ian to approach Scarborough and find out if they could talk to me formally. I didn't want to do anything behind their back. I was quite happy at Scarborough but I said yes to Doncaster, which I wouldn't have done for any other club. My wages went down by £100 a week as I became player-manager. I was given a two-year contract, and knew I had a massive challenge on my hands. I saw it as a great opportunity, even though the club was at a low ebb, virtually extinct. We didn't have any footballs, we didn't have any nets, any kit or anywhere to train. What an introduction to management.

I went to the ground around July 12 or 13 and found only five players still on the books, and that was because no one else wanted them. I could approach other players to see if they'd be willing to come but I couldn't do anything formally until the takeover went through on August 1.

I asked Glynn to join me, but he was due to start working for John Hendrie at Barnsley, and said no. I tried another former team-mate of mine, Billy Russell, and he turned me down. Eventually I recruited John Stiles, the son of Nobby, the 1966 World Cup winner. John was a pal of mine who had been my team-mate at Doncaster and Leeds. We received word on August 1 that we were the new management team and had two weeks to get ready for the start of the season at Dover on August 15.

I dropped my kids off on my first day and walked towards the Portakabins on the car park, which housed the offices. I knocked on the door and a woman opened the window. I said: "Hiya, love. Ian Snodin."

"Oh no, he's not in yet. Apparently he'll be in by 9 o'clock."

"No, love. I am Ian Snodin."

I thought: 'Nobody's got a clue round here.' Then I saw the secretary, Joan Oldale, who had been there when I was a player. She told me she'd been crying with joy when she heard I was to be the new manager.

## DO YOU FANCY A GAME?

At the time Rushden & Diamonds were paying £1,200 a week to certain players. I could only have three players on £400 while the rest had to be £200-£250. It was very difficult to get people to come on full-time contracts for that amount of money.

I couldn't take prospective signings to Belle Vue because it was so scruffy. There were ripped chairs in the directors' room and it stank. I had to take them to hotels or restaurants. If I'd taken them to the ground, there's no way they would have signed for me.

I started by phoning a few youth-team managers and picked up some kids who had been released, among them a couple of 18-year-olds from Barnsley. Tommy Wright, a former Leeds United player, didn't have a club so I took him. I phoned Kevin Sheedy, then reserve-team manager at Tranmere, and he recommended Kevin McIntyre, who hadn't established himself at Prenton Park (he was still playing for Shrewsbury in 2010).

I phoned another former Everton team-mate, Neil Pointon, who was at Hearts. He told me they'd had a young lad who had been released 12 months earlier and nobody could understand why. I eventually tracked this lad down, Mark Bradley, and he agreed to join us.

The day before the Dover game, Bradley arrived on the train from Scotland at 9.05am and I picked him up. He was wearing a big coat and had his bags with him. I hadn't even seen him play but he was going to be in my starting XI the following day.

We drove down the M1 on the way to Dover and met Kev McIntyre at Watford Gap service station. I'd never even seen him so I was searching round, hoping to spot an athletic-looking lad with a bag. Luckily he was wearing a Tranmere tracksuit so I found him. He was starting, too.

## THE FANS FLOOD BACK

I was still suspended from playing because of the red card I received for Scarborough at the end of the previous season. For my first match as a manager, I sat in the directors' box wearing my suit and tie. In the dugout opposite John Stiles was in charge. I decided I would watch the first half in comfort and then join him for the second half.

One thousand Donny supporters travelled down to Dover which, without wishing to sound egotistical, was for me. It was a brilliant turnout.

Mark Bradley gave me a nasty surprise when he stripped off before the game. He was carrying quite a bit of weight, which I hadn't seen under his big coat, but I had no choice – he had to play.

The game kicked off and after five minutes Bradley chased after one of the Dover players – it was as though he was running through quicksand. I was already thinking of bringing him off. After 20 minutes he was breathing out of his backside. I stood up in the directors' box, looked over at John Stiles and the physio, Jon Bowden, who were laughing their heads off, and I screamed: "Get him off." He'd not done a thing for a year and was totally out of condition.

At half-time he was disgusted to have been brought off, moaning, "I'm not happy" when he went to get showered, but he clearly had a belly on him. I decided not to have a go at him because he'd come down and tried for me. We lost 1-0 and it was a brilliant result. Andy Woods performed heroics in goal; otherwise it would have been seven or eight.

On the Tuesday we played Southport at home. I was in the dressing room beforehand trying to pump the players up when there was a knock on the door. It was the chief constable of Doncaster Police. He told me they'd have to delay kick-off and when I asked why, he invited me to step outside. There were queues over 100 yards long of people trying to get in. The attendance was 3,663. We were a breath of fresh air to the Conference. Rushden & Diamonds were the top team and they were only getting 2,500. We took a minimum of 1,000 to every away game.

Ian McMahon introduced a kids for a quid scheme, which was a brilliant idea. For the four or five years before I became manager, no children wore Donny Rovers kits. We had fireworks, music and face painting for normal league games. Eventually we were getting 800 kids through the turnstiles, with parents accompanying them.

## YOU SHOULD SIGN DARIUS VASSELL

After about six games Glynn decided to join me, as the Barnsley job had fallen through. He'd also seen how the town had responded to me taking over. Westferry approached John Ryan, a plastic surgeon originally from Doncaster, and asked him to become chairman. We'd known John for years and he was a massive fan. He guaranteed Glynn's wages.

I employed the son of Alick Jeffrey, a Doncaster Rovers legend. The son, who was also called Alick, ran the bars. Eventually he became commercial manager and did brilliantly, setting up all kinds of sponsorship deals.

There was no scouting system when we started. After a few weeks it consisted of me, Glynn and my dad, who had done match reports for Charlton, Barnsley and Donny under Billy Bremner. He's very knowledgeable about football, my dad.

Three scouts wasn't very many so whilst we were having a cup of tea one afternoon, I asked Alick if he would watch Barnsley Reserves against Aston Villa Reserves while Glynn, my dad and I went to other matches. He was happy to do so. Our kid was sceptical about sending Alick and I attempted to reassure him, arguing: "He'll be fine. His dad played and he was a youth-team player himself. No problem."

The next morning we convened to discuss what we'd seen. I mentioned two or three players, Glynn mentioned a couple and then it came to Alick. He slammed his pen down and exhaled in wonder. "Did I see anything? You've got to get this kid."

"Who is it, Al?"

"He plays for Aston Villa. He's only 18. Darius Vassell."

"You what?"

"Quick as hell, he'd score goals for fun for us."

"Darius fucking Vassell? He's an England youth international. They value him at £5m. He was only playing to get himself fit for the first team."

"I can only report what I see."

"Alick, don't ever go scouting for me again." Glynn, my dad and I were in hysterics.

## ALICK JEFFREY THE 'PSYCHO'

Not too long after my time as Doncaster manager ended in 2000, Alick developed a serious infection that spread to his brain. He was rushed to hospital in a serious condition and operated on. It was a very worrying situation, but he gradually improved and pulled through.

I visited every day. Once he was in a better state, I wanted to try and keep it as light-hearted as possible. He was strapped into a wheelchair and one day I noticed 'physio' had been written on his belt because he was due to see the physiotherapist. He said to me: "You've got to get me out of here."

I replied: "Look, you nearly died. You're in the best place and they're looking after you. You'll be able to leave in a couple of weeks."

"No, I've got to get out – they think I'm crazy. Look what they've written on my belt."

Alick thought it said 'psycho'.

## A MANAGER WHO COULDN'T SUBSTITUTE HIMSELF

In November, we had an FA Cup first-round tie against Southend United at Roots Hall, a Football League team then managed by Alvin Martin. After all that had gone on, it was a big game for us.

I played centre-back with Glynn in charge from the sideline. It lashed down all day and the pitch was extremely heavy. We scored an early goal but at half-time I told our kid that I was absolutely knackered and asked him to take me off when an hour had been played for the benefit of the team. He tried to persuade me to stay on but I insisted that I didn't have much left.

Southend attacked us in waves but we were holding on. I asked the referee how long was left and he told me "20 minutes", 10 minutes longer than I had intended to stay on. I signalled to Glynn that I'd had enough and he put his thumb up. A few minutes went by and there was no sign of any substitute warming up. I gesticulated frantically to Glynn and his thumb went up again.

After a while there was a substitute ready to come on.

However, when the board went up, it wasn't my number. I stood with my arms outstretched and yelled "me". Glynn shouted back: "No!"

I ended up playing the full 90 as we held on for the win. The players were ecstatic in the dressing room, jumping about like over-excited children, while I gave Glynn a massive bollocking. He told me: "You can't beat moments like this – I had no intention of bringing you off."

## AGONISINGLY CLOSE TO A DREAM FA CUP TIE

We played Rushden & Diamonds in the second round. After a 0-0 draw at Belle Vue, the draw for the third round took place and our potential opponents were Leeds United at home. What a dream tie for me, and Donny as a club.

Disastrously, Mark Hume was sent off in the fourth minute of the replay at Nene Park. I gave him a very dirty look as he trudged off. They eventually beat us 4-2 but we absolutely battered them, even with 10 men. Our supporters were right behind the lads, who were fantastic that night. Brian Talbot, the Rushden boss, came up to me during the second half and said it would have been stopped if it had been a boxing match. That was very generous, as we'd had a couple of run-ins during the first game.

If we'd kept 11 men on the pitch, we'd have beaten them and gone on to face Leeds, who finished fourth in the Premier League that season. Managing Donny against a club I had captained would have been a very special occasion.

## CLIFF-HANGER WITH DOVER

Four days after we lost at Rushden, we had a home game against Dover, who had been our opponents on the opening day of the season. It was an incredible afternoon. Their striker, Joff Vansittart, scored a hat-trick within 27 minutes but then had to go off injured. We scored after half-an-hour to make it 3-1. I didn't go mad at them in the dressing room at half-time because I knew we had a lifeline. I tried to gee them up and the dressing room was buzzing – we couldn't wait for the second half.

We got it back to 3-3 and I was giving it loads on the touchline. However, they went up the other end and made it 4-3 with 11 minutes to go. The atmosphere went flat but we came back to win 5-4. Judging by the scenes, you'd have thought we'd won the FA Cup. It was an emotional rollercoaster and a fantastic game to be involved in, one of the best I'd experienced.

## CUP JOY

We eventually finished 16th, which was superb considering where we started. It was almost impossible to manage properly for the first six months, but I absolutely loved the whole experience.

I found it difficult to join in as a player because I had to generate sponsorship and interest in Doncaster, holding meetings with top business people. It was non-stop, 24-7. There was so much to do from day one, a massive rebuilding job. I couldn't keep fit and play. I did turn out a few times, but nowhere near as much as I would have liked. If everything had been in place and it was a smooth operation, I would have played far more often.

I can honestly say that the lads loved the training. Steve Nicol came in for six months and was brilliant for us. Years later he told Glynn that the best training he ever experienced was at Donny Rovers. Apparently once he was out of bed in the morning, he couldn't wait until he got in. All those years he spent winning trophy after trophy at Liverpool and he said that about us. I felt great when Glynn told me.

We made it as professional as we could; local companies ploughed money in, Asics supplied our kit and we restored the club's credibility. For the previous five years you didn't see anybody wearing a Rovers kit, but now they were flying out of the club shop.

We also won the Conference League Cup. For the first two rounds we played fringe players and apprentices because we weren't that bothered – but we got through. Now we were in the semi-finals and everyone in the town was right up for it. We beat Morecambe over two legs, and met Farnborough in a two-legged final.

We travelled to their place first. The attendance was over 2,000 and previously their average was 400. We won 1-0 and just had to avoid defeat at Belle Vue in the second leg. The kick-off had to be delayed again because of the crowd – it was a full house of 7,160, and people were turned away. We ended up winning 4-0 on aggregate. The fans were ecstatic; they were on top of the dugout, there was champagne flying about. It was incredible.

## SEARCHING FOR GOLD

During that first season we signed Dino Maamria, a Tunisian striker. Adrian Heath had recommended him when I was putting the team together. He had a great physique and was very enthusiastic so I gave him a one-year contract. He became a crowd favourite and they would shout "Dino, Dino" if he was left out and they wanted him on.

In September we lost 1-0 at home to Forest Green, despite battering them for the whole game. Afterwards Glynn and I were sat in an office just off the dressing room, wondering how on earth we'd got beat. There was a knock on the door and it was Dino, who had played up front on his own.

"Dino, what do you want?"

(Panicking) "Boss, boss, boss. I've lost my gold chain during the match."

"Dino, that's the last thing on my fucking mind right now. Please. Go and have a word with the groundsman."

"Boss, I need to find it – my wife bought it for me."

"Dino, fucking hell. We've just got beat 1-0 and I'm fucking devastated. I'm not going to go searching for a gold chain."

After Dino had gone home the groundsman found it and gave it to me. Two days later we were back in for training and hatched a plan to wind Dino up.

Alick Jeffrey used to sell fake jewellery on the local market, so we explained to him what had happened and told him to take the chain.

Dino was straight in my office when he arrived for training.

"Boss, boss, has anybody found my chain? My wife says I must find it."

"Whoa, whoa, whoa, Dino. Calm down. We've found your gold chain."

"Oh, boss. Thank you very much."

"The groundsman found it but there's a problem, mate."

"What's the problem, what's the problem?"

"I gave it to Alick to look after and, I don't know if you know, he used to sell fake jewellery."

"No, please."

"I've come in this morning and he told me he sold it yesterday on the market."

"You're fucking joking."

"You'd better go down to his office and see him."

He dashed out and I quickly phoned Alick to tip him off that Dino was heading his way.

A very agitated Dino barged into Alick's office and barked:

"Jeffries, Jeffries. What have you done with my gold chain?"

"Whoa, whoa. Settle down now. Dino, that chain was not yours."

"It was, it was."

"The groundsman told me he found it in the 18-yard box and you never went in there once the other day."

"No!"

Alick immediately burst out laughing and produced the gold chain.

## FLYING JAFFA CAKES

Mickey Walker, who is the director of football at Rovers now, was in charge of the youth team when I was manager. For one game I invited him into the dressing room to observe how Glynn and I worked. I was happy for him to have an input if he wished.

I'm old fashioned where football is concerned. I think you put your kit on, put your boots on and get out there. Our kid's different, he's into pasta and giving them energy and Mickey Walker is exactly the same.

I walked into the dressing room at 1.55pm to read out the team and there were jaffa cakes in plastic tumblers, with loads of bananas laid out. I was mystified and asked Glynn who'd prepared all this food. Mickey piped up and told me that jaffa cakes gave you energy.

We came in at half-time and were 1-0 down after an absolutely appalling performance. I was fuming and made sure I was the first one up the tunnel so I was waiting for the players. They had shown nothing whatsoever.

Mickey was hiding near to the showers as the players sat down. I picked up one of the tumblers of jaffa cakes and booted them. The tumbler split and there were jaffa cakes everywhere. I screamed: "Energy? Why don't you get out there and show some fucking energy!" When I kicked the tumbler one of my trainers flew off so I was walking around the dressing room with a limp as one leg was now shorter than the other.

I was trying to spot this training shoe out of the corner of my eye. After about five minutes I saw it. The lads told me a couple of days later they were dying to laugh but daren't risk it. We went out for the second half and won the game 3-1.

## A TANGO WITH AN OPPOSITION MANAGER

When I was Donny manager, the Conference used Mitre footballs, but we didn't have any supplies for training and warm-ups. A lad called Aiden Butterworth, who had played with me at Donny, was a leading rep at Adidas so I phoned him up and asked if he could provide us with a few footballs. He sent 15 Adidas Tangos, which was great.

Soon after the Tangos arrived we had a home game. Before the match the opposition manager approached one of our apprentices and started moaning about the Tangos, demanding that his team should warm up with Mitres. He said: "Go and tell your manager that I want Mitre balls."

The apprentice was clever enough to go to the groundsman

rather than bother me. The groundsman responded by knocking on the away dressing room door – he explained the situation but still their manager insisted on Mitres. The groundsman told Glynn what was going on and the fact that this pain in the arse wanted me to sort it out. Glynn knew what my reaction would be and decided to knock on the door himself.

The guy said: "Look, I've told the kid and I've told the groundsman: I ain't training with Tangos. Go and tell your brother to come and see me."

I heard about all this and took four Tangos off Glynn. I knocked on the door and the manager came up to me.

He opened by saying: "Ian, I've told the apprentice, I've told the groundsman and I've told your brother – we don't play with Adidas Tangos." He went to shut the door but I stuck my foot in it.

I said: "Look, we ain't got any Mitre balls. We're warming up with Tangos too."

The door was shut and I knocked on it again. One of the players opened it and as he did so, I threw the balls in the air and volleyed them into their dressing room. They ricocheted around like a pinball. I repeated: "Warm up with these and we will play with a Mitre."

"That's out of order," he protested.

"Fucking shut up you," I replied.

It gave me great satisfaction that we went on and won the game.

## BIG NAMES ARRIVE

I brought in experienced players like Neville Southall, Steve Nicol, Mike Newell, Tommy Wright and Dave Penney. For someone like Andy Woods, it was wonderful to be able to learn from Nev. You don't manage people like him. People remarked about his weight but he went on to play for Bradford in the Premier League.

The Donny public had been used to watching amateurs from non-league. Alright, one or two of the experienced lads didn't do themselves justice but it was great for the supporters to see such players six months after the club appeared to be dead.

## SIGNINGS THAT MAKE ME PROUD

When we were building the team at Doncaster, I brought in the goalkeeper Andy Warrington from York Reserves when he was only 19. He's still playing for Rotherham United now. Paul Green, who I signed as a 16-year-old apprentice, went to Derby and they're talking about wanting £2m for him. I feel proud that we brought them to Donny and they're still in the game.

## A FAKE – AND WHY I TRIED TO KICK MY OWN PLAYER

Just as I was taking over at Doncaster, Ian McMahon, was contacted by a guy who spoke with a Dutch-American accent, offering himself to us for a trial. Going by the name of Mason van Basten, he said he'd been playing for Miami Fusion in Major League Soccer and possessed three Dutch international caps.

'Van Basten', who claimed to be related to Marco, said he wanted to come to Donny because he had family living in the town. As soon as Ian mentioned the name to me, my reaction was: "Do me a favour – I'll take Marco but I'm not having him." Ian did offer him the opportunity to take part in a pre-season game at Worksop but to my complete lack of surprise, Mason never showed.

Presumably the guy who spoke to Ian was actually called Wayne Scott, of Plane Close, Doncaster. A man of that name was given a suspended prison sentence in 2009 for contacting a number of football clubs using a variety of aliases, and requesting match tickets for charity prizes after telling hoax stories. In 2003, going under the name 'Jason van der Sarr', he promised to buy York City for £6.5 million before withdrawing the offer. He was eventually exposed for using 20 different aliases at various times, including 'Kane van Basten', 'Michael van Basten', 'Logan Michael van Basten' and 'Logan Michael Wolverine'.

At the start of my second season as Donny manager I was

offered a foreigner who I wish had been fake. His name was Mirsad Bubalovic.

John Ryan, the chairman, told me that an agent had been in touch, offering a Croatian who had been playing in France for Sochaux, having previously turned out for Hadjuk Split and Croatia Zagreb. He said two or three other European clubs wanted him. John was quite gullible were agents were concerned and would take their spiel to heart.

My response was: "John, if that's the case, why does he want to come to fucking Donny Rovers in the Conference?" The chairman wanted to give him a 12-month contract but I protested that I hadn't even seen him play. I insisted on watching him in a training session.

Bubalovic was described to us as a 6ft 2ins centre-forward who was good in the air, strong, quick and could score goals. When he turned up he was about 5ft 10ins and must have weighed no more than 10-and-a-half stone. I shook his hand and introduced myself while the rest of the lads trained. His English was limited.

John admitted to being disappointed by his appearance, but still argued for giving him a six-month deal. I pointed out again that I hadn't seen him play so then he suggested three months. I said no again. John claimed the agent would take him away and I said: "Let him fucking take him away." I wasn't going to be rushed into a decision.

Bubalovic trained with us and showed one or two good touches without looking remotely up to Croatia Zagreb's standard. John asked for my thoughts and I said: "Give him three months." It wasn't going to be much out of my budget so I was happy enough with that arrangement. If he proved to be shit, he could be home by Christmas. The player and agent ummed and ahhed so I told John to palm him off. However, the chairman persisted and eventually a three-month deal was agreed.

The following Saturday we had a home game and I was in the middle of the pre-match team talk 10 minutes before kick-off when I heard the following tannoy announcement:

"Ladies and gentlemen: Our latest signing, one of the greatest players who will ever grace Belle Vue, Mirsad Bubalovic!"

I stopped the team talk in mid-flow and exclaimed: "Fucking what?" I walked out of the dressing room, headed for the pitch and was confronted by Bubalovic in a long leather coat, blowing kisses to the crowd, who were all going mad. I signalled for the tannoy announcer to stop. I was absolutely fuming. The rest of the lads were pissing themselves.

It wasn't long before we found out Bubalovic was earning more than any other player. At the time, we had Mike Newell on the books and only months earlier Steve Nicol. He was also given a car and put up in a hotel.

Bubalovic came on for five minutes in a local cup game against Brodsworth Welfare. That was the extent of his Doncaster Rovers career. He was shit. Weak as hell. It was eating away at me that he was on more than anyone else.

At the time, the players had to take their kit away and wash it themselves. Bubalovic never washed his kit once – he stank. The lads were coming to me and begging me to force him to wash it. I lost my rag big time. I hauled him into the office and shouted: "Your kit – fucking wash it. You stink." He claimed not to understand but he had a selective knowledge of English.

During training, I was trying to kick him. The manager was trying to kick his own player. I didn't want him at the club, the lads didn't want him at the club – they all knew he was earning more money and it was hurting them. Some were asking if they could kick him in training and my reply was: "Fucking do what you want boys." That's how much he got to me. He had conned the club.

Eventually he left the hotel and moved into a house with Joyce and Dave, who had traditionally looked after Donny players. Joyce was a great landlady, the best I'd ever known. Newelly stayed with her a few times and said she was first class. After two weeks she phoned me up and said: "Ian, can you get this fella out of my house? He goes out at 11 at night before coming back at 2 or 3 o'clock in the morning."

It was getting to me even more now. I phoned the chairman

and said: "John, we need to pay this kid off and get him out of the club. He is disrupting training and getting on my nerves. I want to punch him."

There was a young girl called Carla, about 18, who worked on the front desk. She told Joan Oldale that Bubalovic had been stalking her when she was on nights out with her friends. They would move on to another bar and he would follow them, order a coke and stare at Carla. Joan told me all this and it was the final straw.

I spoke to Glynn and told him to send Bubalovic to my office as soon as he turned up for training that morning. I was kept waiting because he never appeared. At 1pm I was in my office seeing to some paperwork when Joan walked in to tell me Bubalovic had arrived and was stood at the front desk, trying to talk to Carla. I got up and headed straight for him.

"What do you want?"

"What do you mean, boss?"

"What the fucking hell do you want?"

"I've come for my mail."

"Mail? Who is going to send you mail? You're never going to play for Donny Rovers again while I'm here. I want you out of the club. You're worrying this girl. Get out of my sight or I'll fucking knock you out. I'm getting on the phone to John Ryan and your agent to get you out of this club."

"You're crazy."

"Yes, I am crazy and you're shit. Get out of my sight."

"I'll have you shot."

I spoke to John and he agreed that we needed him out. His agent arrived, took him away and that was the last I saw of Mirsad Bubalovic. A complete blagger. Needless to say, I am still waiting for him to give it to me with both barrels.

## SACKED

John Ryan had a place in Palma and arranged for us all to have a five-day break in Magaluf at the end of the 1998/99 season. We had a magnificent time and there was a meal scheduled for the last night. A banner erected at the restaurant announced: "Welcome to next year's Conference champions."

I pulled him and said: "Dear me, chairman. It's a tough league and you are happy with us staying up. You're putting a bit of pressure on by putting up a banner like that." He replied: "No, we'll win it next year." I couldn't believe what he was saying.

We were doing alright at about 10th or 11th in the league during 1999/00. However, John and Peter Wetzel, the vice-chairman, thought we should have been top.

One day I went to watch my young lad play for Doncaster Under-14s and received a call from our kid. He asked why I hadn't been answering my phone. I was perplexed and Glynn said that John had been trying to contact me without success. I told Glynn: "My phone hasn't rung once." Glynn responded: "John wants to see us first thing tomorrow at 9am."

I knew straight away what this meant and told Glynn: "We're getting the sack."

"Shut up."

"I'm telling you. We're finished."

I was in for 8.30am the following day and Joan Oldale came through. She absolutely loved us to bits and asked what I was doing. I told her: "I'm getting sacked in half-an-hour." She started laughing and I insisted: "I'm telling you."

It came to 9 o'clock and Glynn and I sat down with John and Peter. John opened up: "Right, gents. I hate doing this. I'm a Rovers fan and you've been heroes of mine but recent results haven't been great. We should be in the top two or three."

I jumped in. "You're fucking joking. Top two or three? You went on video at the end of last season and said what a partnership these Snodin brothers are going to be. You said what we'd done in the first year was remarkable. We had a five-year plan to get back into the Football League and 19 months down the line, you're doing this. This club was a disgrace when we got here."

"Yeah, I know, but we still expect..."

"John, you're talking shit. I know what's coming – I've already cleared my desk – and all that crap about trying to get hold of me...my phone never rang once. Don't lie."

I tried to persuade them to keep Glynn on and make him the manager but our kid said: "No, no. We come as a pair and we'll go as a pair."

I said: "No, I'm telling you: give him the job."

John replied: "We've looked at it and you're both leaving."

I got up and said: "You're a pair of fucking knobs", before walking out.

Glynn tried talking to them so I walked back in and said: "Glynn, you're dealing with two idiots. Let's go."

It should have been a five-year plan. If we'd been given time, we'd have taken them up, no problem. The chairman brought Steve Wignall in after me. I phoned him to wish him all the best and even met up with him to offer advice. They gave him boat-loads of money but he did nothing and got the sack.

I felt bitter about what happened. It was a dream job for me and it hurt for a long, long time – a good year or two. We'll never know what might have happened.

I'm delighted at what the club has gone on to achieve over the last 10 years, finishing 2009/10 mid-table in the Championship. I love the town and I'm always made to feel welcome at the football club. A lot of people have shaken my hand and told me: "If it wasn't for you, we wouldn't be here in the new ground (the Keepmoat Stadium)." That's a huge compliment and I feel good when I hear that.

## THE CHAIRMAN

I get on great with John Ryan now. He loves the club and wants the best for it. He has invested a lot of money. Initially he was trying to get the club to run before it could walk but he has often said to me that Donny could strive to match the likes of Barnsley and Blackburn. I used to think he was a bit off his head, but look where he has taken them.

He did say he'd retire and die a happy man when Donny reached the Championship – but he's still there now.

## WHY I'VE NEVER APPLIED FOR ANOTHER POST

As a man-manager, I could be a right bastard but I could also be their best friend. That's how Billy Bremner was with me. We had a great time in training – the lads would travel from long distances but love the experience when they were out on the pitch.

Even though Sean O'Driscoll has done a magnificent job for Donny since becoming manager in 2006, he doesn't show much emotion when they score a goal. Fans still come up to me and talk about the passion I showed when I was in charge.

If I'm brutally honest, I think John Ryan and Peter Wetzel spoiled my chances of becoming a decent manager. They were close to extinction when I took over and within 18 months they were a good Conference club. I became disillusioned after I was sacked. I've never felt it was worth applying for other Conference or lower league manager jobs. If they looked at my CV, they wouldn't know what state Doncaster Rovers were in. No club at that level could be better than Donny anyway.

Part of me would love to get back into management to show what I can do. I do believe I have a lot to offer to the game but I'm not going to apply for jobs for the sake of it. I enjoy my radio and corporate work and I'm looking forward to establishing a sports management company that will look after young players.

# CHAPTER 8

# TAKING THE MIC

Post-management, I moved into the media. My first live
Everton game featured a slur on the Saint and there have
been plenty of laughs since, including a co-commentator
eating a roast on air, a phone-in fake and yours truly being
'named' one of the Blues' worst players

Is there another job you'd like to do?
*"Not really."*

Ian Snodin, Everton programme 'Player Profile', 1987

## RADIO DAYS AND A MESSAGE FOR IAN ST JOHN

AFTER the sacking, it took a while to get over what happened. I started doing some work on Doncaster games for Radio Sheffield. At first that was a bit strange because I was talking about players I'd brought to the club, but life moves on and you have to go with it.

I'd been Doncaster captain at 18 and had to represent the club so a microphone never fazed me. I soon settled into the radio work.

Out of the blue, Graeme Sharp called me to tell me he was about to give up his Everton commentary work for Radio City in Liverpool to join Century Radio. Sharpy put my name forward as his replacement at City. It'd been such a long time since I'd been back to Goodison that I jumped at the chance.

They gave me a six-game trial. My first commentary was against West Ham at Goodison in December 2000, and it became a famous match.

Paolo Di Canio caught the ball inside the Everton penalty area when the Blues' goalkeeper, Paul Gerrard, was lying injured. What a great gesture that was from Di Canio because he could have easily headed the ball in, or controlled it and tapped it in. It would have been a winning goal as well because the score was 1-1 and it was in the last minute.

In the phone-in afterwards I was sat with the late Phil Easton, who hosted the show, and Ian St John. It was the first time I'd come across Saint and I was slightly in awe of him; not only was he a great player, he'd presented 'Saint and Greavsie' on ITV for years. I was excited to be working alongside him.

Liverpool hadn't played that day so most of the calls related to Everton and I dealt with them. There were many kind words from the fans, saying it was great to have me back on Merseyside before going on to talk about the Di Canio incident. It was like listening to an LP over and over again.

On about the sixth call, the same thing was happening. The guy was in his car, on the way home from the match, greeting me and talking about what had happened with Di Canio. Then he asked if Ian St John was with me. I replied: "As a matter of fact, there's only me, Saint and Phil left in the ground. Why, do you want to talk to him?"

"No, tell him he's a wanker."

It went out live on air because they weren't using a delay button at the time. I thought to myself: 'Welcome back to Merseyside.'

I worked for City for the next few seasons and really enjoyed travelling around, meeting the fans and hearing their opinions. It did always amuse me when people phoned up and said: "We weren't very good today, Ian" when they hadn't even been to the game and had listened to my radio commentary.

I've always said to my radio employers that I won't slaughter the manager or players – I'd pack it in first, especially now that I do corporate work at Everton. One of the first people I see at Goodison on a match day is Bill Kenwright, the Everton chairman, and he is always very friendly.

Bill has had plenty of stick over the last few years but he is great to me. He sent me a wonderful letter when I became manager at Doncaster Rovers and I've never forgotten that. I've got great admiration for him. He's a massive Evertonian, as simple as that. I won't slag anybody off – players, managers, board members or even fans.

## ROAST DINNER AND AN IMPROVISED COMMENTARY

After starting commentary on Everton games, Radio City's sports editor Steve Hothersall received a call from John Bradley of Radio Aire, asking if I could join him to work on Leeds United games when I wasn't covering Everton. It was perfect for me because I lived in Yorkshire and I was looking forward to getting started.

Steve asked if I'd heard about my new commentary partner. I hadn't, and he told me that John was a bit different to the Radio City style of commentary. I questioned what he meant but Steve said: "I'm not going to tell you, I'll let you find out for yourself."

The first match I covered was Leeds versus Liverpool at Elland Road. I met John, a big lad with a big beard, outside the ground.

He asked: "Has Steve told you about me?"

I replied: "No, not really. He just told me that you've got a different style of commentary to the Radio City boys."

He said: "Well, I'll not tell you what it is – you'll see when we get up there."

We went through the preview and the game kicked off. Phil Thompson was Liverpool's assistant manager under Gerard Houllier at the time, and within three or four minutes he was stood on the edge of the technical area, remonstrating with the referee and having a go at his players. I remarked on how animated he was and John Bradley responded by bursting into tune, singing: "Sit down, Pinocchio; sit down, Pinocchio." I looked at him in disbelief and said: "John, you can't say that live on air about one of the coaching staff."

He responded: "Snods, wait a minute. Let me sing that again." Off he went with another chorus of: "Sit down, Pinocchio." I couldn't believe what I was hearing.

It was a Sunday game and at half-time John asked me to fetch him a roast dinner from the press room because he couldn't leave the commentary position. I went down and had mine – roast beef and Yorkshire pudding – while we talked over the first half. It was lovely – you always used to get a great feed at Leeds.

I was a bit late going back up to the commentary position and the players were just about to start the second half when I took my seat. I put the plate down in front of John, who promptly took his headphones off and started to tuck in to his beef. He then announced: "Right, Snods will give you the first four or five minutes of commentary while I eat my Sunday dinner." I didn't have time to argue because he had a mouthful of veg. I couldn't believe what was going on and had to pick it up immediately, saying: "Fowler passes it to Kewell, Kewell on to Viduka..." and so on.

I was happy to summarise but this was very uncomfortable. I was thinking: 'What am I doing here?' John started making satisfied noises and remarking, live on air, about how hot the potatoes were and asking if I'd brought any salt, while encouraging me to carry on with the commentary. I feel sorry for anyone who had to listen to me. When he was finished, he put his 'cans' back on and said: "Oooh, that dinner was lovely" before we were back to concentrating on football for the rest of the match.

In the phone-in afterwards, people were saying to me: "Snods, what's Bradders like, hey?" I had never worked with anyone like him. He'd get up to that kind of thing every week. It was totally off the cuff; he'd talk about American wrestling while the match was going on.

I've become good mates with Bradders since then. I got a shock a while back when I phoned him up and he told me he was working for Liverpool's channel, LFC TV. I don't get to listen to him now, for obvious reasons.

## SNODS' BET

Rob McCaffrey, a good pal of mine, offered me work with Sky soon after they started covering Conference football. Doing TV was totally new for me. I was a little bit apprehensive, but Rob reassured me and explained that he'd talk me through it as the presenter of the programme. I had the option of co-commentary or appearing in-vision for pre-game, half-time and post-game analysis. I agreed to appear in front of the camera.

I had done quite a few games for Sky when they introduced a feature called 'Snods' Bet'. They knew I liked a flutter and decided to show the odds. The first match this feature appeared in was Dagenham & Redbridge at home to Hereford United in February 2004.

Hereford were second-from-top at the time and going really well. Dagenham were 6/4, Hereford 5/4 and it was 11/4 the draw. Rob asked for my pick and I said: "Well Rob, Dagenham have had excellent results recently and they are at home. Hereford are second-from-top but they've lost two out of the last three and they've got a couple of players missing through suspensions. The viewers should back Dagenham at 6/4 – I think they are tremendous value."

The game kicked off and Dagenham had a player sent off for a professional foul after five minutes. It finished 9-0 to Hereford. At the time, it was the most goals ever scored during a live televised game in England. What a way to launch a betting feature. We never did it again.

The following day we covered Woking versus Chester and I had to walk across the pitch before the game. All the Chester fans were shouting: "Snods, Snods, I hope you haven't told anybody to back us today."

## ON AND OFF AIR

Non-league football is a totally different environment; they make you feel so welcome. We were allowed access to places Premier League or Football League clubs wouldn't let you near. I settled into the role, got a lot of work from it and thoroughly enjoyed the whole experience.

I was disappointed when Sky lost the contract to Setanta in 2007. The former Manchester United right-back, Paul Parker, knew the producer and was given a role with them. I am a great pal of Paul's, I've known him since England youth days and he stayed with me when Everton played Man United. He rang me to explain that Setanta were going to use him, which was a great gesture. I said to him: "Paul, that's life. The producer knows you but I got in through Rob McCaffrey. Good luck, mate."

Paul covered the first season but wasn't available for the first couple of games at the start of the following season. He put me forward to stand in, Setanta liked what they saw and they extended my contract to cover northern games, the likes of York City, Burton Albion and Mansfield Town. They thought the viewers would like to hear a northern voice.

It snowballed from there and eventually the games were pretty much split equally between Paul and myself. It was going really well before Setanta went bust in 2009.

## MR SINGH FROM DONCASTER

Covering non-league football led to an appearance on the phone-in show 'You're on Sky Sports'.

I had been in the same house as John Stiles, who had undergone a career change and become a stand-up comedian, when he called the programme to speak to that night's guest Clive Allen, pretending to be an Irish Leeds United fan. He was upstairs on the telephone while I watched it in the lounge. 'Paddy' was talking about David O'Leary and every other sentence included the words "Jesus, be God". You could see Clive Allen looking at Rob McCaffrey and thinking, 'Who is this fella?' I was laughing my head off.

When Rob asked me to come on the show, I was determined to keep it from Stilesy. I knew that if he got a whiff, he was 100% sure to phone in and pretend he was somebody else.

On the day of my appearance I mentioned it to a lad at the local golf club, Steve Shaw, which was a fatal mistake. I bought a lovely shirt from town and looked the part. The driver from Sky arrived and took me down to the studio. Of course, Steve telephoned Stilesy to tip him off.

I got down to London, had my make-up applied and went on the show. Again, it was a bit daunting but I soon settled. There were questions about Everton and Bolton and a little bit of banter. After an advert break, Rob read out a few texts and then announced: "Our next caller is Mr Singh from Doncaster."

I knew straight away who it really was. I'd seen his act and although he doesn't do racist jokes, Stilesy does imitate the Indian accent. I shook my head, while Rob and the producer were wondering what was up with me. I said: "Rob, this is not Mr Singh from Doncaster. This is the son of the famous Nobby Stiles – John Stiles." There was a little giggle and the caller protested, saying: "No, no, no, no, no – this is Mr Singh from Doncaster."

We continued to argue about who he was before 'Mr Singh' went on to praise David Moyes for the job he was doing at Everton. He finished off by saying: "Ian, you were a great player, but I think you've put a bit of weight on now." Rob and I were in stitches.

As soon as we came off air, I phoned John up. The producer was having kittens but I assured him it had been a wind-up. I put it on speakerphone and he answered in an Indian accent.

I found out later that Stilesy had phoned Joanne to double-check I was on Sky, and told her that he would "have me".

## TERRACE TALK AND AFTER-DINNER SPEAKING

I present the preview programme 'Terrace Talk' every Saturday on Radio City with Ian St John. The Saint's 72 now and he's full of opinions. He buys every newspaper every day and he's clued up on everything.

I love working with him and we've got a great show. It's on all year round, although the Saint has a lot more holidays than I do! We have a great rapport, a good laugh and both of us seem to enjoy it. I am obviously biased towards Everton and refer to them as "we". That shows the affinity and feeling I still have.

Commentator-wise, I think Alan Irwin, who covers Everton for Radio City, is excellent and I also like Clive Tyldesley, who was on City himself in the late 1980s when I was playing for Everton. I remember meeting Ian Darke from Sky one night in the Holiday Inn in Liverpool when I was still playing and he had just covered one of our games. I was quite drunk and told him he was an excellent boxing commentator but a shit football commentator. He likes to remind me of this whenever we meet.

Many people don't like phone-ins but I've always enjoyed doing them. I like to hear other people's opinions and have a bit of banter. When I started I did used to listen to every point and answer them all. Now I will give the producer the 'cut' signal when they're waffling on too much.

I also do a bit of after-dinner speaking. I only do them around Merseyside, North Wales and Chester because most of my stories relate to Everton. I love doing them, though. It's great to tell the stories and get a reaction from people in the audience. I love it all – TV, radio work and after-dinner speaking.

## CONFRONTATION WITH PHIL THOMPSON

I commentated on a derby game at Goodison in August 2003 and Liverpool had beaten Everton 3-0. As a fan, I was annoyed but that's part of the game. I've been on the winning side and, if you're involved, you are absolutely over the moon and shout and celebrate. I don't mind players doing that but managers and coaching staff should be a little bit more reserved.

Phil Thompson is a Liverpool lad and has been part of the club all his life so obviously it's going to be a big thing for him when they beat Everton. From my time as a player, I remember Howard Kendall and Colin Harvey would react to a derby win by shaking hands on the pitch, getting down the tunnel and celebrating in the dressing room.

In this case, Phil celebrated on the pitch. He was kissing his badge and pumping his arms. I happened to say that I thought he was out of order and that a member of staff should be a little more dignified. I could see one or two people were getting annoyed at his actions and suggested he should celebrate in the dressing room. Someone must have told him what I'd said.

The night before the Anfield derby later that season, I stayed in the Marriot Hotel in Liverpool city centre. I came down for my breakfast on the Saturday morning and, after my feed, was heading for the lift to go up to my room to get changed.

As I did so, I saw Phil and the Reds' centre-half Sami Hyypia walking towards me – I didn't even know Liverpool were staying there. I put my hand up and said: "Hiya, Phil" but he started wagging his finger and told me: "You were fucking out of order."

I thought there was somebody behind me and turned around. When I saw there was nobody there, I queried him: "Me?"

"Out of order."

"Why? What's your problem?"

"I've been looking for you for months. What's this you've been saying about me on the radio – kissing my badge and inciting a riot?"

"You were out of order."

As the lift doors opened, Phil followed me in. As the doors

shut, he started to go on about the number of derby games I'd played in, telling me I didn't know what it meant because I wasn't born on Merseyside...it was a load of nonsense. I was getting annoyed and started effing and blinding and was half squaring up to him. Then the lift doors opened and he got out. I was shouting insults as he walked down the corridor, before the lift took me to a higher level.

I was still fuming as I changed my clothes and prepared to leave. When I was coming down in the lift, it stopped at the same floor where Phil had got out earlier. I thought, 'Oh, please be Phil Thompson.' The door opened and he was standing right in front of me. He said: "I'll take the stairs" and as the door shut I shouted: "Yeah, fucking do one."

I didn't see him for ages afterwards until I did a dinner in Kirkby, Phil's hometown, and he was in the audience with one of his sons. By this time he had mentioned the incident in his autobiography and it had caused a bit of a stir. I went straight up to him and said: "This could be interesting, couldn't it?" He shook my hand and said: "Look, that's forgotten now, let's get on with it."

## SCOUTING

I finished commentating for Radio City when I was offered the position of chief scout for Luton Town in 2005 when Mike Newell was in charge. I did miss covering Everton, but I enjoyed my new role.

Luton were drawn to play Liverpool in the FA Cup third round in 2006 and I had to prepare the match reports on the opposition ahead of the game. It takes a good 10 hours to do, covering all their corners, free-kicks and the general shape of the way they play. Before I provided the proper version, I decided to send a fake one, based on the Liverpool side of the 1980s. I had Bruce Grobbelaar in goal, Phil Neal at right-back, Alan Hansen at centre-back, Jan Molby in midfield with Kenny Dalglish and Ian Rush up front.

In my comments, I said Molby had "terrific pace and was up

and down, non-stop for 90 minutes, a real box-to-box player". For Kenny Dalglish: "His first touch is horrendous, always gives the ball away, don't worry about him because he's overrated." Ian Rush: "Slow and misses several chances." Mike read the report to the Luton players in the dressing room and they all burst out laughing.

Luton had a decent side at the time and it was great working with Newelly. He has excellent ideas on the game and all the lads loved playing for him, as well as his training and his philosophy on football. He might be too honest for his own good at times, but he should definitely still be in the game.

While I was at Luton, I still lived in Yorkshire and generally worked from home, going down there once or twice a week. When Mike left, Kevin Blackwell replaced him. I don't know if he was testing me out but soon after he took over, he asked me to travel to a reserve game at Portsmouth where they were playing West Ham. I was fuming, but kept my mouth shut and travelled all the way down to the south coast.

Harry Redknapp and Paul Hart were at Portsmouth at the time and asked what I was doing. They told me they'd sent a memo out, explaining that they were fielding an under-18 team. Within minutes I discovered West Ham were playing under-18s too. I didn't really know any of the players, apart from Mark Noble. Harry and Paul told me to go home and said that if anyone asked any questions, they'd say they'd seen me. I saw the kick-off and drove straight back to Yorkshire. It wasn't long before the inevitable happened. I said I wanted out and Kevin got someone else in. That was me with Luton.

After I left the club, I was offered the opportunity to rejoin Radio City. I co-presented 'Terrace Talk', the Saturday preview programme, as a stand-in before taking on the role full-time alongside Ian St John. I wanted to do commentary initially but the more I do the show, the more I enjoy it.

## WORST EVERTON PLAYER WIND-UP

Four Four Two magazine ran a feature about every club's best and worst players a couple of years ago. Ian St John had been mentioned among Liverpool's best so, during Terrace Talk, I spoke about the complimentary things they had written about him. Saint then read out the Everton list. He told our listeners I had been voted among the top 10 worst players to represent Everton. Apparently I couldn't tackle and had no pace; the article also expressed astonishment that Everton and Liverpool tried to sign me. I was stunned and lost my rag on air.

They showed me the article and I didn't know what to say. We had loads of texts from Evertonians defending my honour. I was really wound up and couldn't concentrate as I tried to discover who wrote the piece. Unknown to me, somebody had mocked up the page and stuck it into the magazine. It was a massive wind-up and I bought it. It looked totally genuine.

# CHAPTER 9

# *SNODS ON*

I've always been partial to a flutter, whether it be horse racing or Wacky Races. I helped to get a jockey drunk on Grand National day with hilarious consequences, while a well-fed greyhound proved to be a record-breaker. Sometimes I had success, sometimes I got burnt...

**Your best sporting moment outside football?**
*"Backing a 33/1 winner at Doncaster Races"*

**Ian Snodin, Everton programme 'Fact File', 1987**

## A BET THAT BURNT

MY dad always liked a bet on a Saturday afternoon. When I was a kid, horse racing bored me but that changed as I got older. I'm now more than happy to spend afternoons in William Hill's or Ladbrokes.

At Everton, a few of the lads liked a bet. It was nothing too extravagant but with Kevin Sheedy and I, who are the best of mates, it got a little bit ridiculous in terms of what we would bet on.

When we went on tour, we'd bet on whose bag would be first off the airport carousel. It started as £10 on our first trip but then it mounted to a £50 wager. Occasionally, and unknown to me, he'd get Kevin Ratcliffe to stand at the front and if he saw my bag before Sheedy's, he'd lift it off and put it back on once Sheedy's had gone past.

We went to Hawaii at the end of the 1986/87 season for five days and had a £100 bet on who would get the best tan. On the first day I lathered myself with sun cream, but Sheeds claimed he didn't need any protection. He lay out in the sun for two hours and ended up severely burnt – he was in agony. I was laughing because I thought he wouldn't be able to leave his hotel room for the rest of our stay. I demanded he pay up there and then but Sheeds was adamant that we wait until the last day and compare tans.

Quite a few of the lads went out surfing while Sheeds recuperated and I joined them. I was out in the sea for three hours with no cream on. I ended up in a worse state than Kev, burnt to a crisp, in agony.

The pair of us had to go to the doctor to get a special cream to try and ease our pain. We called a truce in the end.

## WACKY RACES

Relaxing in a hotel room one afternoon before a night game, Kev and I watched the cartoon *Wacky Races* on the tele. We each picked a character and staked £50 on who would cross the finishing line first.

Sheeds chose Professor Pat Pending and I picked the Ant Hill Mob. The cartoon was on for 20 minutes and for 18 of those minutes, the Ant Hill Mob was winning. I was rubbing my hands, having a right laugh. Now and again the Professor would come into the picture but then drop back. Sheeds was counting his money out, ready to hand it over to me.

However, Dick Dastardly had put some glue a yard from the finish line and the Ant Hill Mob became stuck, with the nose from the car about an inch from the line. All the other cars also became stuck but the Professor flew above the glue and crossed the line first. I think we both said "no more" after that because it was getting out of hand.

## DAN THE MAN

Not too long after I joined Everton, Kevin Ratcliffe had his testimonial season and one of the events was a 'do' in Lydiate, on the outskirts of Merseyside. I was told there was going to be a horse racing trainer there. I was thinking Henry Cecil or Michael Stoute but it turned out to be a guy called Mike O'Neill, who trained horses in the area. Ratcliffe introduced us. We talked away for a little bit but I'd never heard of him.

By the end of the night I was very drunk and had my arm around a sober Mike O'Neill, telling him what a great trainer he was. He wanted a few of the Everton lads to lease a racehorse called 'Dan the Man'. He drove me home and then called me the next day to talk about it.

When we were back in training, I talked to the lads. Ian Wilson, Kevin Sheedy, Neil Pointon, Dave Watson and myself agreed to get involved. Forty pounds came out of our monthly wages and went towards the training fees. I used to call in to the yard quite regularly. We'd be stretching and warming up and even Colin Harvey would ask: "Snods, how's Dan this morning?" It was the talk of Bellefield.

Sheeds and I had both been to the yard a few times when Dave Watson asked if he could go. When he did, there were 45 horses in the stable and 44 of them were trying to kick the doors down, raring to go. Sadly, Dan the Man was sprawled out, fast asleep and snoring. Waggy came in the next day, told us all this and said: "I don't think it's got much chance." Still, we got a great buzz from talking about it.

In contrast, Ian Wilson thought we had a horse that was going to run in the Epsom Derby or at Royal Ascot. He asked if we would need to hire a top hat and tails. I told him it was more likely to run at Market Rasen.

It was supposed to run one afternoon at Pontefract and we were planning to shoot up there after training to watch its debut at 2.05pm. However, at 11am we received a phone call from the travelling head girl to tell us it had injured a leg in the horsebox while it was being transported to the racecourse.

We'd receive a monthly receipt of the costs, on one occasion 19 pence for an injection. It became laughable. As there was no return for our money, the lads became fed up after a while and didn't pay the bills. Sheeds received a threatening letter, saying that if the outstanding costs weren't paid, he'd never be able to own a racehorse in this country.

It never raced but for four or five months, every morning, the question was: "How's Dan?"

## JOVEWORTH? NO CHANCE

After our first drunken meeting, I got to know Mike O'Neill very well and had breakfast with him on the morning of the 1989 Ayr Gold Cup along with Jimmy Fortune, who was his jockey at the time, and a couple of stable girls. They had a horse called Joveworth running in the big race that afternoon. I asked Mike if it had a chance and he told me: "It's like a bog up there. It's been raining for three days and Joveworth doesn't like heavy going. It can cope with good-to-soft at the max. The conditions are against it – it's not got a prayer."

I backed something else. Neil Pointon drove me into training in the afternoon and I asked him to stop at the William Hill near Fazakerley so I could check the result.

As soon as I walked in, I could see Mike O'Neill and Joveworth on the television screen. Joveworth was wearing a blanket declaring him the winner of the Ayr Gold Cup. Jimmy Fortune was sat on top, punching the air and acknowledging the crowd. I couldn't get my breath – it had won at odds of 50/1. I had only been with them that morning and they told me it had no chance.

I walked out with a dazed expression on my face. Kevin Sheedy, who was also in the car, clocked this and wound the window down.

He said: "No, it hasn't?"

"Yes."

"Joveworth?"

"Joveworth's won the Ayr Gold Cup."

"What price?"

"50/1."

That just shows that you can never be sure of anything in racing. If the trainer genuinely doesn't think a horse has a chance, how can punters know any better?

## "WHIP THE F*** OUT OF IT"

In the summer of 1992, the Scottish striker Alan McInally was given a trial at Everton having suffered knee problems while at Bayern Munich. He only knew fellow Scot Maurice Johnston but his outgoing personality was immediately obvious as his singing voice filled Bellefield.

On his second day with us, Alan joined Maurice, Mark Ward and myself as we headed to Haydock races. We had become quite pally with the jockey Peter Scudamore because his son, Tom, was an Evertonian. When Scu knew we were attending this particular meeting, he told us that the owners of the horse he was riding in the last weren't going to be present. He suggested we could represent them and got us access to the paddock.

We were straight on the drink when we arrived and by the time of the last race at 5.30 we were bladdered. Scudamore was a big hero of McInally's so he was very excited at the prospect of meeting the great jockey and acting as the owner of a horse he was riding.

We lined up for a photograph before the race with the trainer, Martin Pipe. I happened to be stood by Scu until I was shoved out of the way by McInally, who promptly put his arm around him. He then started to instruct Scu how to ride this horse. "For the first circuit I want you tucked in behind on the inside rail. Three fences from home I want you to move forward and then, two from home, hit the front and whip the fuck out of it." In fairness, Scu started laughing straight away, even though I'm sure he didn't have a clue who McInally was.

We all put a few quid on 'our' horse but it finished no better than sixth.

## A BET ON THE BLUES

I've only once wagered money on a match I was involved in – and for a while it looked like I was going to be responsible for losing the bet.

Mike Walker had just taken over as Everton manager in January 1994 and we weren't playing very well. Our opponents for his first home game were Swindon Town, who were awful and bottom of the league. We were evens to beat them. I thought, 'If we don't beat these, we don't deserve to win another game.' I gave my mate £1,000 to bet on us.

The game began and before too long we were 2-0 up. We were absolutely strolling it and I was looking forward to collecting my winnings. They pulled it back to 2-1 early in the second half, despite having a man sent off. Soon after, I received the ball at centre-half and thought I had plenty of time as I looked for an option. As I did so, Paul Bodin, the Swindon full-back, took the ball off me, ran on and slotted it past Neville Southall to make it 2-2.

The crowd was having a go at me and I was thinking about my thousand quid. It was going to be my fault – I could have cried.

Eventually we went on to win the game 6-2 and it turned out to be the easiest thousand pounds I'd ever earned in my life. As I said, that was the only time I ever bet on us, and there's no way I would have ever bet against my own team.

## GETTING A JOCKEY DRUNK

I was in a hospitality tent at Aintree one year on Grand National day and the Liverpool midfielder Jan Molby was also inside, enjoying the refreshments with me. We were drinking champagne and having a good time.

I'd got to know Steve Smith Eccles, the jockey, reasonably well. He was due to have just the one mount on this occasion, in the first race. His horse finished nowhere so I invited him to come and join us afterwards. He happily accepted.

Steve was having a few drinks with us as the afternoon progressed. The last race was approaching when there was an announcement over the tannoy: "Can Steve Smith Eccles please come to the weighing room?" We suggested that he might be needed for the last race but Steve thought it unlikely. Off he went, telling us he'd be back shortly.

He returned five minutes later, wearing silks with a whip and boots. Jenny Pitman's jockey had been injured in the penultimate race and Steve was his replacement. The horse was the second-favourite too. We were laughing our heads off. Then he merrily announced: "Anyway boys, tally ho!"

We were glued to the television screens waiting for the race, desperate to see how Steve got on, given what he'd put away. The commentators were saying that the horse had a very good chance and would definitely stay the distance.

Off they went. All the horses cleared the first fence okay and we were getting excited, shouting: "Go on, Stevie boy." Then they reached the second. The commentator said: "Oh, there's been a faller – it's Steve Smith Eccles on the second-favourite." We were in bulk. When we saw the replay, it hardly touched a twig. The horse jumped the fence almost perfectly, it just stumbled slightly on landing and Steve slid off to the side. He came back in after the race and said: "How I got over the first, I'll never know."

## ANDY KING AND THE GANGSTER

Andy, an Everton midfielder of the late 1970s and early 1980s, hosted a corporate hospitality tent one year at Aintree. He asked for a few of the Everton players to attend in support so Graeme Sharp, Dave Watson and myself went along.

There was a local gangster inside, wearing a trilby and an overcoat. Kingy was holding court, there was food and drink and everything was going really well. However, we didn't know that this gangster was several thousand pounds down after the first few races. We weren't betting extravagant amounts but we were winning. Dave had £20 notes stuck to his collar and coming out of his ear. We were making comments about how easy this gambling lark was. We weren't taunting anybody, simply having a laugh. However, the gangster wasn't very amused.

It came to the last race of the day, by which stage he was apparently £10,000 down. We were all bevvied, including Kingy. As the race was coming towards its conclusion, the gangster's horse was in the leading three. If it won, he was going to pretty much break even for the day.

With two fences to go, the gangster remained quiet whilst the rest of us were shouting at the screen. At this moment Kingy walked up to the tele and turned it off. The gangster barked out an order, brooking no argument: "Kingy, get the tele on NOW!"

An increasingly frantic Andy couldn't get the race back on. He was panicking while the shouts of "NOW Kingy, NOW!" came from the gangster. He just about managed to get the picture back on 100 yards from the winning post. Luckily, the gangster's horse won and he had a smile on his face. Kingy put his arm around him. The gangster said: "It's a good job my horse won, Kingy. This could have been the last corporate event you ever did."

## FEED THE GREYHOUND

While horse racing has long been a big interest of mine, the same can't be said for greyhounds. However, I did become involved in the sport, briefly, a few years ago.

I was friendly with Francis Jeffers, the former Everton striker, who had a big pal called Tommy. Both of them were keen on greyhound racing. Tommy asked me if I'd ever been to Askern, an independent dog track close to my home where, apparently, Jack Russells and Great Danes would get a run.

As I hadn't, Tommy wanted me to take a fast dog he'd recently bought for £5,000 to the track to get it graded in a time trial. He explained that he would give the animal a big feed beforehand to slow it down. The plan then was to race it again without a heavy stomach, and clean up when it won. He told me: "If they hear a scouse accent, they'll smell a rat so you make out your part-owner. I'll stand 100 yards out of the way."

I met Tommy on a Sunday afternoon. He brought the dog in a van and said: "She's a little beauty but it's not going to be quick today – she's had a full English breakfast, everything except black pudding." I went along to Askern, accompanied by a mate from Doncaster who knew a bit about the sport. My mate was doing the talking when the track owner approached me and introduced himself, saying: "Hey up, Ian. I didn't know you were into dog racing." I waffled on about trialling it and not knowing whether it was any good.

What looked like a bin liner was sent around the track and the traps opened. Our dog stumbled out and off they went for one-and-a-half laps. After the short sprint, we retrieved our four-legged flyer and gave it a drink. Tommy approached and was very excited, saying: "Did you see it stumble out of the traps? The time must have been shit. We'll get it graded really low and come back to clean up – it's a little machine this, you know."

The owner came over to me again and said: "Ian, that's not a bad little dog. It stumbled out of the traps though."

I replied: "I know – it's done that a few times."

"You can't run it here any more."

"Why not?"

"It's just broken the track record."

Tommy came over and asked what was going on, so we told him about our little record breaker. His response was: "You're fucking joking? It had a bigger breakfast than me this morning."

The track owner offered £2,000 for the dog. Tommy admitted he'd paid £5,000 for it and said: "Fair enough, you got me."

"Good one for trying," the track owner replied. "Now you and the dog, fuck off back to Liverpool."

## MY BETTING STRATEGY

I'm a traditionalist. I don't bet anything online; I love to go to race meetings and into betting shops. I love Aintree and Chester in the north-west and I love Yorkshire meetings as well. Doncaster is right on my doorstep and York is not too far away. It's a good day out but it can get you in a lot of trouble as well so you've got to be careful.

I like my football coupons too but I never bet on Everton. I like to relax and enjoy the game when I'm watching the Blues, I don't want the worry of thinking about a bet I have had on the outcome.

# CHAPTER 10

# AT THE BAR

Shy, retiring, teetotal – I'm none of these things. I've always loved a social occasion and more often than not, alcohol has been involved. This has led to fun and games all over the world, including Magaluf, Mauritius, Dublin, Bangkok...and the Fishermans Rest, Southport

*'Ian doesn't drink that much during the week, but admits a partiality to lager and lime after a successful match'*

**Daily Mirror, '21 Things That Made Snodin A Glory Boy', 1987**

*"I've been training every day, even on my holidays in Florida. Someone said you put on weight in Florida, but I lost seven pounds and I feel great. I've been running every day, watching what I eat and keeping off the alcohol"*

**Liverpool Echo, 'Why Ian Snodin's just a shadow of his old self', 1992**

## DRINKING CULTURE

I WASN'T really an excessive drinker before I came to Everton. I liked a social with the lads on a Saturday night, but nothing out of the ordinary.

When I moved from Yorkshire to Merseyside it became obvious that not only were they a fantastic football team, they were also top of the table in the drinking stakes. I became one of them. You have to get to know your team-mates and the best way to do that is to socialise.

Other clubs were still drinking a lot from the late 1980s and into the '90s. Everton were notorious for having a drink but it was rare for someone to step out of line.

As a team, we socialised within reason. We did used to drink hard but when it came to training, we were fantastic. We were athletes but we knew how to let our hair down. I can't see anything wrong with that, as long as it's in moderation and you're not doing anything completely stupid.

It's completely different now. Players will have the odd drink but nothing like what we used to put away. When they do go out, it tends to be private places where they are well looked after.

Looking back, I went out too much when I was injured. I had my reasons because the hamstring wasn't getting better but you can see on photographs that I put on quite a bit of weight.

## CHRISTMAS CHEER

On Christmas Day 1988 my wife's family visited. We were due to train at Bellefield that evening before a game at home to Middlesbrough the following day. I remember great intentions not to drink.

However, at the lunch I had a couple of beers. The couple of beers led to another couple of beers and then another couple of beers. I'd never done it before and never did it again. It was just one of those stupid things where the family came down and I got involved in drinking and it went on and on.

That evening Kevin Sheedy and Graeme Sharp arrived at my

house in a taxi to pick me up, before we went to Neil McDonald's place and then on to Bellefield. When they arrived at mine, I was bevvied out of my head. I refused to go with them while Joanne tried to talk sense into me. There was a bar in my dining room area and I was getting everybody drinks. She had to go out and tell Sheedy and Sharp that they needed to come in and get me.

I offered them drinks while they said: "Come on, we've got to go training now – get in the car." Eventually I staggered in and started singing songs and Christmas carols. The lads were discussing how they were going to hide my state from Colin Harvey, a tough task given how loud and boisterous I am when I've had a drink. When we reached McDonald's house, I walked in, wished his family a merry Christmas and helped myself to another beer.

The lads said it was hilarious. They were sat in the car thinking, 'Look at the fucking state of this.' I would never advise anybody to do it.

We arrived at Bellefield and Sheedy and Sharp pulled Peter Reid straight away to tell him I was bevvied. We were only due to have a light session featuring a game of head tennis, so they decided to have me on their team to attempt to hide the drunken reality. They kept the ball between them, not allowing me to get involved and demonstrate my impaired coordination.

I should have let them get on with it but obviously my thoughts were not rational at this point. I was shouting for the ball and they were telling me to shut up. Colin was refereeing the other game – he must have heard me and must have known I'd had a drink. Next we were running from one end of the indoor pitch to the other. We were meant to touch each wall before turning in the opposite direction but I missed with my leg and headbutted the wall. The lads were pissing themselves.

We got to the hotel and they made sure I was straight to bed. I got up the next morning, felt great, had my breakfast and got plenty of water down me. I then gave one of my best performances in an Everton shirt. The lads said to me afterwards: "Fucking hell, you want to go out drinking more often." I was outstanding, playing one-twos, overlapping and whipping balls in.

## MAGALUF

We went to Magaluf a few times under Howard Kendall, Colin Harvey and Mike Walker. I know it like the back end of my street. We'd tend to go for five days at the end of the season and there could be about 30 or 40 different teams out there at the same time.

In the first few years most of us would get up in the morning, have a bit of breakfast and start drinking from 9-10am. It would be midnight before people would start to drift back to their hotel rooms. Most weren't too bothered about going to nightclubs; we'd rather have a good day out in the sun.

I'm not much of a sleeper so I'd tend to be up no later than 8am. On one of my first trips I walked down to the beach bar and Howard was already there, in his flip-flops, having a little gin and tonic. The atmosphere was brilliant every day.

Howard would go every year. In 1996, on the day Manchester United beat Liverpool in the FA Cup final, there were a load of Geordie lads surrounding him, asking for photographs because he was from the north-east. Howard had the biggest cigar I'd ever seen; it must have been a foot long and looked like a rolled-up carpet.

Virtually the whole squad would go in the first few years. We'd worked hard all year and wanted to let our hair down. The manager was in charge if anything went wrong but it was generally every man for himself.

I remember seeing Shaun Garnett when he was at Tranmere looking absolutely gorgeous during a fancy dress day. He was wearing a yellow dress, lipstick, a blonde wig and high-heeled shoes.

## ON THE RUN FROM COLIN HARVEY

Jimmy Martin, the coach driver/kit manager who I mentioned earlier, came to Magaluf with us on a couple of occasions. One

**Butter wouldn't melt:** Glynn and I, in more innocent times (above) and in tasteful red (right)

**On the run:** I'd gone from the halfway line to score this one against Halifax Town in October 1983, and (left), an early 1980s Doncaster photocall with the moustache gathering pace

**Progress:** Above and left – With England U21s in Turkey, 1984 (back row, third left) in a team including keeper David Seaman and future Everton team-mates Paul Bracewell and Trevor Steven (front row second right and right); below, in Leeds United action, 1986

**From the scrapbook:** With Glynn ahead of my Everton debut against my brother's side, Sheffield Wednesday, at Goodison, January 1987

**Everton & England:** In 'B' action (above), and with 'Eusebio's shirt' (left)

**Duck:** Avoiding Neville Southall's flying fists at Arsenal, 1990

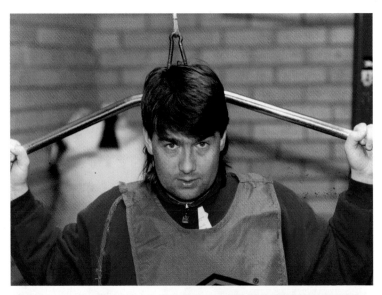

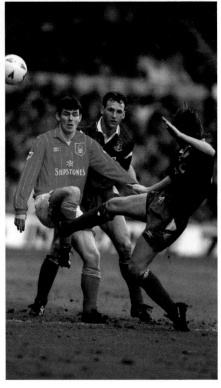

**Comeback:** Looking to get back to my fighting weight in the gym (top and above); making only my second start for nearly two years, in a 1-0 win at Nottingham Forest, November 1992 (right)

**Highs and low:** Wimbledon v Everton, January 1993 (top) – a post-war record low attendance of 3,039 witness my final league goal; I celebrate in front of the ball boy in awful salmon pink (left); captaining the Blues in 1993/94 (above)

**Beginning of the end:** Left – A handshake for Mike Walker in his first game as boss, a 1-1 FA Cup draw at Bolton, 1994; (bottom left) my final game at Goodison Park, v Leicester City, September 1994; on loan at Sunderland soon after (below)

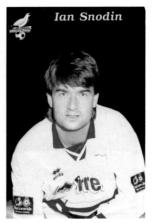

Ian Snodin

**Moving on:** In action for Oldham (left) and a shot from my season at Scarborough (above); suited and booted in my first season in charge of Doncaster (below), with physio Jon Bowden also prowling the touchline

**Pensive:** A look of concern from the Doncaster Rovers' bench

**With the boss:** Below – Promoting an Everton 1980s book with Howard Kendall

morning myself, Graeme Sharp, Neil Pointon and my Everton-supporting pal Ronnie Galvin were inside the Coach and Horses pub at 8.30am. We were having a bacon sandwich and a bottle of Bud for breakfast when we saw Jimmy walking past wearing a t-shirt, a pair of shorts and trainers. He looked like he'd had a good bevvy the night before.

We invited him inside but he shouted "no", because he didn't want to start drinking so early. The bacon butties were held in the air and we hid the bottles of Bud, at which point he decided to join us. We let him into our booth while ensuring he was stuck in the corner and couldn't get out. A bacon sandwich was ordered for Jimmy...plus a bottle of Bud. He protested, but it was too late.

Jimmy was due to meet the managerial team of Colin Harvey, Terry Darracott and Mike Lyons for a run at 9am, followed by a swim. He was insistent that he had to go but we were dismissive, telling him to enjoy his holiday. Within an hour he'd had four or five Buds and was saying "fuck Colin – I'm not going for a run or a swim."

By 2pm the table was full of empty Bud bottles, we were singing and having a great laugh. Who walks past but Colin, Terry and Mike. Jimmy dived under the table and pleaded: "Don't tell him I'm here."

Colin came in and remarked on how early we'd started drinking. I asked him: "Have you seen Jimmy Martin?" while pointing to below the table. Colin winked and carried on the conversation.

"No but when I see him, he's in fucking trouble."

"Why?"

"We go for a run every morning at 9am. We made a pact before we came out and he's not turned up. I'm telling you, when I see him, he's in for it big time. I'm going to tell him to get on the plane and get home."

Then I said: "Are you going to tell him, Jimmy?" He was shushing us from below but I announced: "He's here."

Jimmy sheepishly crawled out from underneath the table and

said: "Hello boss."

"Where have you been?"

"They trapped me in the corner. I told them I had to run. I wanted to come."

I butted in: "Two hours ago you were saying "fuck the gaffer".

We let him out from the booth and pinned him down. Terry Darracott ripped Jimmy's shirt off his back, took his shorts off and stripped him to his undies. He was instructed to go back to the hotel. We gave him a few pesetas but initially none of the taxi drivers would take him.

When he eventually returned, fully clothed, Colin was laughing away. Jimmy had thought that he was in serious trouble.

## A POINTLESS TAXI JOURNEY

After a day on the sauce in Magaluf, I was paralytic and decided I'd had enough at 3am. I ordered a pizza from a takeaway and mentioned to Neil Pointon that we needed to get a taxi. There was a queue of about 30 taxis and Neil told me there was no point because our hotel was 30 yards away.

I was adamant that I was getting in a cab so I walked up to the vehicle at the front of the queue and asked for the Hotel Guadalupe. The driver pointed to the hotel and protested but I insisted he take me. Pointon tried to pull me out of the car but without success. He set off walking, the taxi went around a roundabout, we got stuck at traffic lights and Neil got to the hotel before me.

## SCOUTING AND A STABBING

During the two years I was absent from the team, from 1990-1992, Howard Kendall knew I was feeling low and did his best to lift my spirits. At one point he asked if I fancied doing a bit of scouting for him, which I was pleased about. If I never made it back as a player, which looked a distinct possibility at one stage, scouting could have been a new role for me.

One of my tasks was to watch Dean Windass in March 1991, who was playing for Hull City and aged 21 at the time. Howard said he'd heard good reports about him and asked if I would go to Port Vale to watch him. The tickets and a car park pass were arranged and I was all set.

In preparation, I decided to have a night out on the Friday. Kevin Sheedy was injured so I asked him if he fancied joining me. Everton were due to play in Southampton on the Saturday so Kev told his wife, Debbie, that he would be travelling to the south coast with the squad and having a fitness test down there. In reality he was having a night out with me and staying over in a hotel before we went to the Port Vale-Hull game together.

It was an absolutely magnificent night and both of us were paralytic. We were dog rough the next morning and when we were making our way to Port Vale, I felt absolutely shattered.

After a bite to eat, we took our seats in the directors' box at Vale Park. For the first 20 minutes nothing happened. I fell asleep. Sheedy gave me a nudge and exclaimed: "Oh, what an effort!" I jumped up and spluttered: "What? What happened?"

"Windass – he beat four players, cut inside, curled it and it clipped the crossbar." I grabbed my pen and paper and started scribbling some notes for Howard. As I did so I began wondering why there wasn't more of a reaction from the crowd, and Kev admitted he had been kidding me along because I'd dropped off.

The game didn't improve much so there wasn't a lot to report. Sheeds and I left the ground 10 minutes early, as all scouts do, and we discussed how Debbie would want to know what happened in the Southampton-Everton game. We listened to the car radio and discovered that we'd won 4-3. Sheeds was panicking, listening to the details of the match, frantically jotting down who scored and in what minute.

We arrived back in Southport and went for a couple more drinks before Kev went home. As soon as he got in, he rang me because he'd lost the slip of paper on which he'd noted down the happenings in the Everton match. Between us we were able to piece together most of what occurred and Kev managed to blag his way through it.

To add to the drama, on the Sunday we heard there had been

a fatal stabbing in Liverpool in the early hours of the morning. We realised that we had spoken to the victim, a pub manager, at the Fifth Avenue on Paradise Street during our Friday night out. We'd discussed Everton and our injurie. Sadly, a little over 24 hours later, he was killed in the pub where we met. The police announced they were looking for people who had talked to him in the previous few days to come forward. This was a problem for Kev as he was supposed to be in Southampton, so we kept quiet and didn't contact the cops.

Kev and I would often go out on a Saturday night and at 10pm he'd tend to head home because Debbie had ordered a Chinese takeaway for them. Graeme Sharp would often leave at 11pm but Neil Pointon and I would stay out.

Occasionally Sheeds would reappear in the nightclub two hours later, announcing his return by tapping me on the shoulder. Debbie is deaf in one ear so if she fell asleep with her good ear on the pillow, he'd go downstairs, climb through the window and head out for a few more drinks. If she woke up before he returned he would be in for a big bollocking.

Kev and Debbie are divorced now. We were all really good friends and are still in contact to this day. I love her to bits; she's a cracking woman.

## THE FISHERMANS PEST

For those of us who lived in Southport, one of our favourite haunts was the Fishermans Rest pub but there was one occasion when we made ourselves very unpopular with the regulars.

Maurice Johnston, Mark Ward, Neil Pointon, Graeme Sharp and myself were joined by Ronnie Galvin for an all-day session.

We went to Joe Farley's Chinese restaurant in Southport for a nice meal in the afternoon and everyone was having a good time. That was until some friendly banter between Maurice and Wardy got out of hand. Maurice threw a glass at Wardy, who ducked out of the way. They were having a go at each other and it all got a little bit naughty. Joe, another big Evertonian who knew all the players, told them to behave and it all settled down.

We decided to move on to the Fishermans Rest, a quiet little boozer where we'd often do the quiz night and have a game of pool. Peter Beardsley, a great mate of mine, joined us for the quiz – he was known as 'Ceefax' and knew everything about everything. By the time Peter, who was teetotal, turned up we'd been out for five hours and were rather loud. He was a bit embarrassed by our behaviour.

We'd answered a few questions before a debate began over one of the answers. Peter was filling in the sheet but I'd had enough so leant over, snatched the paper from him, screwed it up and announced: "Forget the quiz". Peter protested because it was the only reason he'd come out.

Meanwhile, a bit of pushing and shoving broke out between supporters and spilled into the toilets. Sharpy and Ward were involved in the altercation. I went over to try and sort it out and the disturbance soon settled down.

Immediately after this happened, Mark Ward walked past me and I thought I heard him say to Ronnie Galvin: "It's got nothing to do with you." I was mistaken but didn't realise this when I said: "Wardy, what are you having a go at him for? Have a go at me rather than him."

Wardy snapped and threw a punch at me. I immediately threw one back. We ended up rolling about on the floor of the pub during the quiz, knocking hell out of each other. The landlord phoned the police. When they arrived, we were taken into the car park and the policeman gave us a severe talking-to and told us that we were a joke. He was quite right – a few drinks had got completely out of hand. The officer made Peter responsible for getting us home so eight of us tried to pile into his BMW. There was no room for Ward, who decided to lay on Beardsley's bonnet.

The following day there were stories in the press about what had happened. The club reprimanded us and rightly so – we were bang out of order and it was embarrassing to read about our antics. We all returned to the pub to apologise.

## BIKE-RIDING WITH BIG NORMAN

Norman Whiteside signed for Everton from Manchester United in the summer of 1989. He arrived with a formidable reputation as a player and a drinker.

Norman did well for us when he was fit, but his knee problems meant he soon joined me on the sidelines.

The physio, Les Helm, tried to keep our spirits up but as time went on it became apparent that Norman was more or less finished because his cartilage had gone. We spent a lot of time together and not always in the gym.

Les decided to buy some mountain bikes and encouraged us to cycle from West Derby village to a gym owned by a well-known bodybuilder, Terry Phillips, in Knowsley. We would do a circuit there before cycling back.

I felt like I had half a chance of returning to the side so I took the gym work seriously. The first time we got on our bikes, some Liverpool fans passed us in a car and gave us a bit of stick. Norman gave them the V-sign and they whipped the car around and set off after us. We hid in a shop doorway.

There was a pub close to Liverpool's Melwood training ground called The Princess that we passed on our route. It was run by a former boxer and mad Evertonian, Brian Snagg, who we got to know really well. We were riding past it at 10.30 one morning when Norman said: "I don't fancy it today, let's just go for a pint in The Princess." I wasn't led astray but Norman knocked on the door and Brian let him in – there were already about 15 people in there. Norman, in his Everton training gear, took his bike inside, leant it against the bar and ordered a pint of lager.

Off I went to Knowsley. I had been gone two hours and by the time I returned Norman must have had about eight pints. He was playing dominoes and had brown sauce on his face from eating a bacon sandwich. He mounted his bike as we returned to Bellefield and it was hilarious watching him attempt to stay upright.

He must have pulled the same stunt two or three times. I could understand why because he knew he was finished. He was a great lad and one of the best players I played alongside.

He was renowned for what he could put away with Bryan Robson and Paul McGrath when they were together at Manchester United. Norman told me that one Sunday they had 27 pints of Guinness each. McGrath and Whiteside were out of action for days afterwards but Robson trained the next day and was in the top two or three when the United players went running.

## DUBLIN AT THE DOUBLE

During his second spell in charge, Howard Kendall took us to Dublin for three or four days before we moved on to a castle-hotel in Donegal for another few days. We'd loved it in Dublin, having a drink and a laugh, and didn't want to leave.

When we arrived in Donegal we found a golf course and beautiful surroundings by the hotel, but many of us were not impressed by the tranquillity. We didn't even want to go down the drive. There were shouts of: "Turn around, driver – take us back to Dublin." Howard had heard it all before, telling us to "shut up and get on with it".

As we disembarked, I told the driver not to go anywhere because we intended to head back to the Irish capital. Discovering that the room I was sharing with Graeme Sharp was tiny only hardened my resolve. Six or seven of us convened an impromptu meeting and I was elected spokesman. I approached Howard in reception while he was having a coffee with Colin Harvey. He initially refused my request to "have a word" but I persisted.

"The lads want to go back to Dublin."

"No."

"You can't even swing a cat in my room."

"I knew you'd come down, I knew it would be you."

"It's not only me, there are seven of us who feel the same."

"Well, go back and tell your little army we're here for three days. It's lovely and you'll be playing golf."

"You're out of order."

"You're out of order – get out of my sight."

The driver departed and we all had faces on while we ate tea. Next morning the discussion still centred on how we could return to Dublin. Norman Whiteside said he had a well-known friend in Ireland, Gerald Kean, who could fly us out. Meanwhile, Howard was rubbing it in, stretching his arms and remarking how beautiful it was. My considered response was to say, "it's shit". He told me to shut up again.

After breakfast, Howard came over to us and said: "Right, get back to Dublin. I don't care how you do it but if you misbehave and cause any trouble for this club, you are fucking in for it, big time." A few lads, the likes of Neil McDonald, Stuart McCall and Peter Beagrie, were happy to stay, relax and play golf. About seven of us decided to go back and Sharpy suggested chartering a plane. It worked out at about £230 each so we headed for a little airfield about two miles from the hotel. Off we went for three more great nights.

## BOB THE POLE

Robert Warzycha, who was Howard Kendall's first signing in his second spell, was a great lad and a good player. In one of his first games at Elland Road (in the Zenith Data Systems Cup) he was absolutely brilliant.

On his first visit to Ireland, 'Bob the Pole' hardly knew a word of English. By the end of the trip, he had learnt the phrase "Jack Daniels and coke". While we were over there, Howard Kendall came down one morning and asked: "Good night, Robert?" He looked horrendous and when he pointed to Sharpy and me, Howard knew he must have been suffering.

## POINTON'S LADYBOY

During one pre-season, we were in Bangkok after playing Thailand's national team. Neil Pointon was not long divorced. He'd been with his ex-wife since he was 16, and had never been with another woman.

Graeme Sharp and I decided to set him up with a ladyboy

because we were convinced he wouldn't notice the difference. While we were in a bar we got on his case, telling him to get himself a woman. Neil wasn't interested.

There were a few girls knocking about and we knew one of them was a ladyboy. To be fair, he/she was very attractive. I beckoned him/her over and said: "Excuse me: my friend has been through a hard time, will you go and speak to him?" He/she sat down on Neil's lap and started stroking his hair. We sent a couple of drinks over and Neil looked stricken, desperately wanting his new companion to leave him alone.

I said to him: "Neil, you've never had another woman. This is something you've got to do, it's a new part of your life."

He replied: "Not in here, not now. I'm not ready for this."

"Look, is she attractive?"

"Yes, she's very attractive."

"Just buy her a drink and see how the night progresses."

By this stage Sharpy was biting his knuckles. As attractive as the ladyboy was, it had a huge Adam's apple and fingers that were a lot bigger than mine. I was sure Neil would notice at some point but they were getting friendlier and Pointon started to whisper into his/her ear.

I wanted to tell him, but Sharpy kept saying "just another couple of minutes". Before long Neil announced he was going back to the hotel. I said: "Nah, I don't think you should."

"What do you mean?"

"It's a man."

"You what?"

"It's a fella."

"What are you on about?"

"Neil, it's a fucking man that's been sat on your lap for the last half-an-hour."

Neil threw the ladyboy off him and called us "a pair of bastards".

The bouncers were quickly over to throw us all out.

## HOWARD GOES UNDER

In the early 1990s, we played an exhibition game against Aston Villa in Mauritius on an end-of-season trip. It was a beautiful place, the match was played in the first couple of days and we then had about five days to relax and enjoy ourselves. There was the opportunity to water-ski, snorkel and do some deep-sea fishing.

On one morning the captain of Air Mauritius introduced himself and invited Howard Kendall and myself to a 'do' he and his wife were hosting. It was going to involve a 15-minute boat ride across the Indian Ocean to their villa, where there was to be a buffet and drinks laid on.

The other lads had gone fishing so we were delighted to be asked. The captain said they'd pick us up at about 12pm.

Howard and I met at 11.30. He said to me: "Imagine us getting picked up in a big boat – wouldn't all the lads be jealous if they saw us walking up the steps?"

We sat there, anticipating our luxury transport: me with a glass of wine, Howard with a glass of champagne and a cigar. Magnificent boats were sailing past. Amongst them was what looked like a yellow canoe with a motor boat at the rear. I jokingly said to Howard: "There's our boat."

"Fucking good one, son," he replied.

As it approached, it dawned on us that the man on board was the captain of Air Mauritius. We didn't want any of the lads to see this but I had told Peter Beardsley we were leaving at 12 and he turned up to wave us off. He was in hysterics.

Once we arrived at the villa, it was beautiful. We could have any drink we wanted, the food was magnificent – there was lobster, king prawns and all kinds of seafood. You could tell they were a wealthy couple. We talked to the other guests and really enjoyed ourselves, becoming quite drunk. As 7pm approached we knew we would have to leave to join the rest of the squad for our evening meal.

Another couple were in the boat for the journey back, but they quickly jumped in the water. They asked if I'd join them but I was petrified of the sea and declined the invitation. They said: "Come on. Look, we're stood on the sea bed." As much as I'd had to drink, I didn't fancy it. I put my hand in the sea and it was lovely and warm so I put aside my fears and dived in. After a minute or so I realised there were no sharks about and began to feel confident.

I tried to persuade Howard to do the same, but he refused because he couldn't swim. I said: "You don't need to swim – I'm stood up on the sea bed." The boat was about 20 yards from where I was stood when Howard changed his mind and jumped in. We didn't realise that the water was much deeper at that point.

Howard went straight down, out of sight. I started laughing because I thought he was messing about. He reappeared on the surface and desperately tried to scramble aboard the boat. Then he went down again. I realised this was serious and swam across, as did the other couple. The three of us attempted to hoist Howard into the boat where the captain and his wife were trying to pull him in. Eventually we got him in and all he could say to me was "you bastard".

Howard asked me not to say anything to the lads but as soon as we got to shore I told the story. It's hilarious to think back to it now but it was very scary at the time. He nearly drowned.

## I WANT TO GO HOME

On my last pre-season with Everton in 1994, we headed for Sweden. I injured my ankle on the first day, it swelled up and I was put on crutches. I said to Mike Walker: "Please, gaffer, send me home. I'm the fittest I've been for a long time. If I stay out here knowing that I can't do anything, I'm going to drink. Send me home so I can get treatment and do gym work." He refused: "Snowy, I need you here for team spirit." I begged to be sent home but he wasn't having it. My last words were: "On your head be it."

The people who had organised the trip on Everton's behalf were young lads, around 27 or 28. I was out with them from day one, drinking every night. On one occasion I went into a pub/restaurant and, unbeknown to me, Mike and his assistant, Dave Williams, were inside. I was off my face, knocking back slammers and shouting: "One hundred and eighty!" while we played drunken darts. Walker and Williams appeared, saw the state of me and immediately ordered a cab to take me back to the hotel. It appeared almost instantly but I refused to get in. They manhandled me into the taxi, crutches and all, and sent me on my way.

During that tour, there was also a shocking example of full-frontal nudity from an unlikely naturist.

The lads were preparing for a training session when Neville Southall realised his kit had not arrived. All he had were his gloves and boots. He shouted to Jimmy Martin: "Jimmy, if my gear is not here in 10 minutes I am going out there bollock-naked." There were about a dozen people dotted about, waiting for the boys to start the session. I decided to encourage Nev by saying, "you won't do that", knowing full well that he would. When his kit didn't appear in the allotted time, he put his boots and gloves on and headed off to the training pitch in his birthday suit. I was in hysterics. That was Nev to a tee – once he set his mind on something, no-one was going to stop him.

# CHAPTER 11

# A SPORTING LIFE

**Football may be my first love but I have plenty of sporting interests. I've caddied on the European golf tour, led a future Olympian in a cross-country race, worn the white rose of Yorkshire CCC and scored a century for Everton when the Blues were wearing whites**

*'Apart from Seve Ballesteros, he'd like to meet Geoffrey Boycott and Alex Higgins...A keen cricketer, he had trials with Yorkshire: "There was never any chance of me becoming a Geoffrey Boycott"'*

**Daily Mirror, '21 Things That Made Snodin A Glory Boy', 1987**

## RUN OUT FOR SLOW SCORING BY DAVID BAIRSTOW

I'VE always been keen on other sports, whether it be golf, cricket or badminton. Most sportsmen have good coordination and are quite decent at other disciplines. I was no exception.

During the summer I was a regular at Headingley to watch Yorkshire in county cricket matches. I knew the likes of Martyn Moxon, Kevin Sharp, David Bairstow and Arnie Sidebottom, all stalwarts of the team in the 1980s. I was welcomed into the dressing room and became particularly pally with Martyn, who happened to support Everton.

In 1988 he asked me if I wanted to play for Yorkshire in Sidebottom's benefit match. My response was "too right". Martyn explained that, for whichever Yorkshire player was receiving a benefit in that particular year, Michael Parkinson would host a golf day in Maidenhead before a posh reception in the evening and a cricket match the following day.

I was very excited at the whole prospect, particularly wearing the white rose. What an honour for a proud Yorkshireman. After the golf, I was introduced to the legendary chat show host and sunk a few pints before the night do, which was held in a marquee on the cricket pitch.

It was a black tie job. The Yorkshire players were sat at individual tables with guests who had paid good money to be there. The entertainment came from an opera-cum-blues singer called Marilyn Montgomery. I'd never heard of her and though I was told she had an incredible voice, I did think "it's not my scene, this".

When Marilyn started singing, I leaned over to Kevin Sharp, who was sat two tables away, and said: "Sharpy, I can't sit through another hour of this. Let's get a drink." He told me to shut up but eventually three or four of us did retire to the bar while she warbled on.

There was an auction of various sporting items and I carried in an autographed Arsenal football, which someone bought for £300. The bar was situated at the entrance to the marquee and, towards the end of the evening, the fella who'd made the winning bid walked in with this ball. Sharp knew I was drunk and bet me a tenner that I couldn't keep the ball up 10 times. This should have been easy but I got to eight and dropped it. I called for "double or quits" but lost control again. All the Yorkshire lads were laughing. "Call yourself a footballer?" they mocked.

Before long a game of football broke out in the bar and spilled out on to the cricket pitch. It was midnight and there was dew on the grass. Within 10 minutes all the signatures had been wiped off the ball.

I got to bed at 3am on the day I was going to represent Yorkshire against Maidenhead, who were a decent side. It was a baking hot day, there was a big crowd and I was hungover.

Yorkshire batted first and I went in at number four, which I thought was a touch generous. Moxon and Sharp opened while I padded up, nervous as hell. We were about 100-1 after 10 overs, spanking it around the park and making it look easy, when we lost our second wicket. It was my moment of truth.

I was announced over the tannoy as Yorkshire's next batsman, walked to the middle and took my guard. The bowling was quite swift and although my defence was in good shape, I was struggling to hit it off the square. I had been batting for 25 minutes and had only made it to three not out. There were slow handclaps and shouts of "get on with it" from bored spectators.

At the fall of another wicket, David Bairstow came in as the new batsman and whispered in my ear: "Get a fucking move on." He was on strike and prodded one down, shouting: "Yes, Snods, let's go!" I set off but he stood his ground and barked: "No, go back." By this stage I was halfway down the wicket and stranded. The lads were in hysterics – they had told Bairstow to purposely run me out because of my slow scoring.

## TON UP

In my first few years at Everton it was traditional to play a cricket match every pre-season. In the first summer I was there (1987), we travelled to Wirral to take on New Brighton.

The boys correctly suspected I'd love the sport because of

being from Yorkshire and were very keen for me to play. I was more than happy to do so.

As with the Yorkshire-Maidenhead match, I was due to bat at number four. There was a great crowd with loads of Evertonians present. It was all set up for a cracking afternoon.

Not all of our players were fully up to speed with the rules. New Brighton batted first and one of their men hit the ball towards the boundary and over Neil Pointon for six. It landed in a big bush and Pointon thought it was still in play. He picked the ball out of the bush and started celebrating a 'catch'. We had a mixture of really good players, such as Peter Reid, and some that were ropey to say the least.

New Brighton eventually scored somewhere between 180 and 190. We replied and very quickly fell to 2-2. I came out and faced the last two balls of an over from a quick bowler. There was a bit of banter about me being from Yorkshire as I took guard. I played my first ball confidently and the wicketkeeper chirped up: "Oh, we've got one here. He can play a bit." I got off the mark with two before they removed the fast bowlers from the attack – they could see the game wouldn't last long as many of our men couldn't cope with extreme pace.

With lesser bowlers on, it was easy runs for me but wickets were still falling. Before long I was in the 90s and although we were eight down, we had an outside chance of winning. The fast bowlers were brought back on. I reached my century and raised my bat to the crowd. Getting a hundred is a great feeling, no matter what level you're playing at.

Terry Darracott was the ninth man out and Mike Lyons came in as the last man. We still needed 20-odd. I tried to stay on strike and reached 128 with five runs still required. The fans were right behind us, shouting "come on, we can do it". Then I was bowled. I was absolutely devastated and New Brighton were running about as though they'd won the Ashes. Lyons put a consoling arm around me and said: "Fucking hell, what a knock, lad." The crowd were giving me a standing ovation and Terry Darracott greeted me by saying: "You wanker – you cost us the fucking game." When I asked him if he was serious, he burst out laughing, gave me a kiss and said: "Top innings".

## A YORKSHIRE BIRTH

When our second child was born in 1988 only boys born in Yorkshire were allowed to play for the county cricket club. Our first child was a girl, Zoe, and she was born when I was at Leeds. When Joanne was pregnant for a second time, I told her she would have to go back home to give birth. When she asked why, I explained my reasoning and she told me to "get a life". I got my way, though, as she was back in Yorkshire three months before she was due. I was delighted when a boy came along but, sadly, Ian never showed any interest in cricket.

## LEADING PETER ELLIOTT...AND SEEING HIM CRY

When I was a teenager, I ran against Peter Elliott, who was also from Rotherham and later became one of Britain's best middle-distance athletes, winning a silver medal at the 1988 Olympic Games. Everybody knew he was going to be a magnificent runner from an early age.

As I've already mentioned, I hated cross-country or long-distance running. For that reason I was an appalled 14-year-old when our teacher insisted that the football team had to be part of the running squad for a particular race. I was fine over 100 metres but detested anything longer. I went home in a mood, looking for a bit of sympathy, but dad told me to stop moaning and get on with it.

On race day I teamed up with a mate called Stephen Walker, whose nickname was 'Banjo' for some reason. It had been raining for three days before the race so conditions were very muddy. There were a load of boys in Rotherham Harriers gear, obviously serious athletes, among them Peter Elliott who was in the local paper virtually every week. We were just mucking about, having a laugh.

When the race got underway, Banjo sprinted into the lead, taking everybody by surprise. I was in hysterics. In the early stages we had to trudge through woods and the ground was pure sludge. Banjo and I slid down the bank while all the runners were tip-toeing about, desperately trying to stay on their feet. We were now comfortably in the lead.

The lead didn't last long. After half a mile we came to the steepest hill I'd ever seen. We didn't even attempt to run it. As we walked up, Elliott sprinted past us. I'd never seen anything like it.

Peter was incredible and remained unbeaten in cross-country races throughout school. His final school run took place at Thrybergh Comprehensive, which I attended. It was a big occasion. Camera crews from Yorkshire Television's Calendar news programme were present as he prepared to make history.

Predictably, he raced into a massive lead but one of the school's fifth-formers, a race marshal, deliberately sent him the wrong way. Loads of people were waiting expectantly at the finish line and they were astonished when the leading runner began to emerge in the distance and it wasn't Elliott. Then the second-placed runner came through, the third, the fourth...still no sign. Eventually he appeared, in tears, and finished last.

## A LONG NIGHT NOT HAVING A DRINK WITH JOHN PARROTT

A few days after I signed for Everton, I went to Pontefract races with Joanne and met John Parrott, the snooker player and Evertonian. He came up to me and said how pleased he was that I'd signed for the club, and that he would be happy to provide me with tickets to any of the big snooker tournaments.

We became good pals and I went to see him play Joe Johnson in the UK Championship in Preston in 1990. He was 7-1 up and it was the best of 17 frames. I spoke to John and said I would head up to watch him finish Joe off before we went for a few drinks.

I was sat on my own in the Guildhall for the evening session and the auditorium was quite empty because it was one of the early rounds. The score went from 7-1 to 7-2 to 7-3 and then 7-4. I became twitchy because I was dying for a drink. I caught John's eye on a few occasions and encouraged him to get it over with but the comeback continued. Eventually the score was locked at 8-8 and they were into a deciding frame. It was now past midnight. John won but was so shattered that he couldn't go for a drink. This was not what I wanted to hear after sitting on my own for five hours. I still like to remind him of that long, long evening.

## POINTON HITS 148 – AT GOLF

I could never afford to join a golf club when I was growing up but I always loved the sport. I think I would have played off four or five when I was about 15 or 16 if I'd had a handicap.

While I was at Everton I was invited to a big golf day but couldn't play because of my hamstring injury. I asked Neil Pointon if he fancied standing in. He was reluctant because he'd only played on a couple of occasions and wasn't particularly good. I said I'd walk around the course with him and give him some guidance. Eventually he agreed to play.

When we arrived at the venue, Pointon was a bag of nerves. There were plenty of people watching, which Neil had never experienced before. One of the players in our group was a member of the Black Abbotts, comedian Russ Abbott's band, and he played off two. There was another guy who played off four and someone else who played off eight. Neil wasn't remotely close to that standard. I introduced him to his team and explained that he wasn't a regular golfer. Their faces dropped – they were clearly taking this competition very seriously.

We walked to the first tee and there was a car park 90 degrees to our left, full of lovely, expensive motors. Pointon saw this and started panicking but I thought there was no way he could hit it in that direction. I reassured him: "Neil, it's humanly impossible to hit the ball in the car park from here."

When he was introduced on the tee I was already laughing because of how nervous he was. He pulled away from his stance and asked the announcer to tell me to stop. By this stage there were tears rolling down my face and my shoulders were shaking. His playing partners were not impressed.

Neil followed my advice and used a four iron rather than a driver for safety. He swung the club and hooked the ball...straight into the car park. It hit a vehicle and ricocheted into a ditch. He teed up again for what was now his third shot. He topped it but at least it went in the right direction, down the fairway. However, by the time he'd played seven shots he was still not on the green.

The second was a par three and he left his tee shot 50 yards short. I advised him to use a wedge and take a practice swing. When he did, he made a divot about a foot long and six inches deep. He apologised again before finishing with a six, which made it 16 shots over the opening two holes.

We got to the third hole and he hit a decent tee shot. For his second, he took an iron out and aimed for the green. The Black Abbott (BA) was stood square on to Pointon, which unsettled him. Neil asked him to move and the guy shuffled five yards further forward. Unfortunately Neil's shot was wild and went straight towards the BA, who had to dive on the floor to avoid decapitation. It only just missed his head.

Neil and I were laughing our heads off. The Black Abbott was in a black mood. He jumped up, covered in mud, and said: "This isn't working and I don't think it's very fucking funny."

Neil said: "Look, mate. I'm very sorry but this is only the third time I've played. I will get better."

BA: "No, I'm not having it. Retire yourself."

Me: "You can't do that."

BA: "Well, either he walks in or I walk in."

Neil: "Come on, let's walk in."

Me: "Let him fucking walk in. Look, did you struggle when you started?"

BA: "Yes."

Me: "Well, he's only just started."

BA: "But I was six, not 25 like him."

After a bit of an argument we came to an agreement and everyone carried on. Neil eventually went round in 148.

Pointon still plays to this day...and he hasn't got any better.

## SOUND ADVICE FROM A HERO

My dad idolised Geoff Boycott and I followed in his footsteps. I loved watching him open the batting for Yorkshire. When I was at Everton, I took part in a golf day in Leeds and was waiting to play a shot from the fairway on the third hole. I had a seven iron in my hand and saw a familiar figure approaching – Sir Geoff Boycott. I couldn't carry on because I was so excited. I stopped the shot and introduced myself.

"Hello, Mr Boycott. Ian Snodin."

"I know who you are. Great move going to Everton, son. What iron have you got?"

"Seven iron."

"No. Eight iron. Play it right onto the banking and it will roll onto the green. This is my local course."

The seven iron went back in my bag, I followed his instructions and it stopped five feet from the pin. He shook my hand and said: "What did I tell you?" The man is an absolute legend.

## THREATENING A PROFESSIONAL GOLFER WITH A RAKE

Ian Garbutt, a former professional golfer from Doncaster and a good friend, asked me to caddie for him at the 2004 Diageo Championship at Gleneagles.

He had been on the European Tour since the early 1990s, having won the English Amateur Championship. When I was Rovers' manager he used to train with us. If he was playing in a tournament nearby, such as at The Belfry or the Forest of Arden, I'd go along and watch him, so I was very excited when we got to Gleneagles. The likes of Darren Clarke and Lee Westwood were taking part; it was a big tournament. Sky heard about my new job because I was broadcasting for them at the time so they filmed us and gave Ian a bit of publicity.

In reality, I was more of a bag carrier than a proper caddie. He measured all his distances and chose which clubs to use. Beforehand I spoke to a couple of the caddies on the European Tour and they gave me some advice. For the first two rounds we played alongside Marc Warren, a Scottish lad. Marc's caddy was

John Wilkie, who used to work for Sam Torrance. John was into football and horse racing so we soon struck up a rapport. He said he'd look after me and take care of the raking if Ian went in any bunkers.

Ian only found sand twice during the first round and shot 71. When he did, John threw me Marc's ball to clean and raked the bunker. The second round followed a similar pattern with John doing the raking on the rare occasions my man was bunkered.

In the third round Ian's playing partner was Pierre Fulke, a Swede. His caddie was a very tall fella known as Maori Mick who was not as approachable as John. I said to Garbutt: "Do us a favour, mate; don't go in any bunkers."

Needless to say, his first shot of the third round went straight into a fairway bunker. During the first nine holes, he found sand on eight occasions. He was having a torrid time and I couldn't believe what was going on.

The trap he landed in on the ninth hole was massive, the biggest on the course. Ian reached his ball and it was lying badly under the lip, which meant he had to chip it to the other side of the bunker without actually getting it out. I must have been in the trap for four minutes, raking the sand. They all had to wait for me on the 10th tee. I eventually carried his bag up a hill to reach them, by which stage I was absolutely fuming.

Ian gave me the hurry-up and I reacted by saying: "Garb, if you go in any more bunkers on the back nine, I'm going to whack you over the head with the fucking rake." We were all laughing. Anyway, he didn't find sand again for the rest of the round and I put that down to me threatening to hit him with a piece of gardening equipment.

Ian retired in 2009 and now works for Andrew 'Chubby' Chandler's ISM Management Group, who look after Rory McIlroy, Darren Clarke, Lee Westwood and Ernie Els.

## CHAPTER 12

# *FINAL THOUGHTS*

I've had a great time in football since I made my first-team debut over 30 years ago. In that period I've witnessed incredible changes to the sport: some have been beneficial, many have not

*"He could have walked into the great Leeds side"*

**Billy Bremner, Doncaster Rovers/Leeds United manager, 1985**

## WEMBLEY

IT'S one of my biggest regrets that I never participated in a big occasion at Wembley. When I was at Everton, I was injured for the 1987 Charity Shield, 1989 FA Cup final, 1989 Simod Cup final and 1991 Zenith Data Systems Cup final. A few months after I left in 1995, they reached the FA Cup final again and beat Manchester United 1-0, so that was another day on which I missed out. Playing in an FA Cup final was what I dreamed about as a kid. The two big things you want to do are to play at Wembley and play for your country. I had both taken away from me.

It was only whilst compiling this book that I discovered that I have appeared at Wembley – in a Football League Centenary Tournament in April 1988. Apparently we played Wolves and Manchester United in matches that consisted of two halves of 20 minutes. It's a measure of how significant this event was that I have absolutely no memory of it whatsoever!

## WATCHING THE CUP FINAL AS A FAN

I was at Wembley for the 1995 FA Cup final – sat behind the goal with the Blues' fans. I went with my son Ian, who was seven at the time, and my dad.

I could have watched it with ex-Everton players or through a corporate ticket, but I wanted Ian to experience the occasion with the supporters. I recall walking under a tunnel close to the ground with a pub to the right and thousands of Evertonians swarming all over the place. In an attempt to remain anonymous, I lifted my collar up but, almost inevitably, I was spotted. A few hundred fans ran over towards us; they sang my name and rubbed my head. It was a great feeling and once we were in the ground, fans continued to greet me and shake my hand.

Before kick-off I told Ian that now was the time to visit the toilet because it would be chaos later. He told me he was fine. Come half-time he inevitably announced: "Dad, I need to go to the toilet." This meant another trip through thousands of

Evertonians. Again, I put my head down and collar up; I managed to get in and out of the toilet without a soul clocking me but as soon as I went back into the concourse I was recognised. The fans rushed over, sang my name, ruffled my hair and patted me on the back. I had the little 'un in my arms to protect him but I was being crushed and started to panic. Luckily, four policemen saw what was happening, came over and ushered us away from the madness, back to our seats. It was a wonderful reception but a scary experience. Ian received the biggest bollocking of his young life.

## DESTINATION EUROPE

I wasn't able to play in any European fixtures for Everton because of the ban on English clubs that existed at the time. Happily, I have travelled to the club's away UEFA Cup ties in recent seasons and there have been plenty of memorable moments.

The trip to Nuremburg in November 2007 was the best of them. There were thousands and thousands of Evertonians everywhere, all decked out in blue and white. When I was dropped off by coach at the stadium before the game, I slipped off the pavement and knocked into two fans wearing Nuremburg's red and black colours. I apologised and two scouse accents cheerily greeted me: "Snowy! How are you, lad?" They had acquired tickets by pretending to be Nuremburg supporters and decked themselves out in the German club's hats and scarves. The things fans will do to watch their team. Brilliant.

The atmosphere throughout the whole trip was fantastic. It showed how much European competition means to Evertonians. You don't realise as a player the things that people go through to get to the game. It is a case of planes, trains and automobiles. As a player, you are flown in, you go to the hotel, you train, play and go home. It can take fans days to get there and days to get back. I find it incredible.

During these European trips, I entertain corporate guests on behalf of the club. When we played Norwegian club SK Brann in February 2008, Kevin Ratcliffe, Graeme Sharp, the chief executive Robert Elstone and myself were among a group of seven who took part in a question and answer session the day before the game. All the drinks were free because Everton were picking up the bill. When the Q&A finished, we headed for a pub in Bergen. It was Ratcliffe's round so he went to the bar and ordered four pints of lager, two vodka and cokes and a vodka and tonic. It came to £74. It was my round next so I thought: 'Oh my God'. I quickly downed my vodka and coke, checked the lads' pints and saw that they'd only had two or three sips. I asked: "Anybody ready for a drink?" They said no and it was only Robert Elstone who wanted another one. My round was a bargain at £15. After a while Ratters realised what I'd done, tapped me on the shoulder and said: "You bastard – typical Yorkshireman."

## FROM EVERTON TO ARMTHORPE

I haven't played much football over the last decade. In August 2000, a few months after I had been sacked by Doncaster, I was contacted by Des Bennett, a former Donny team-mate who was then (and still is) the manager of Armthorpe Welfare, of the Northern Counties East Premier League.

As I'm a good friend of his, he asked me if I would play for Armthorpe. Given what had just happened to me, I told him it was the last thing I wanted to do. He persisted and, eventually, I agreed he could register me, on the proviso that he could only call me up if he was really desperate. The local paper picked up on my 'signing' and it caused a stir. People were coming up to me and saying: "Fucking hell, you've gone from Everton to Armthorpe."

I did make one appearance for them in 2002/03. They had injuries and suspensions and had reached desperation point. I was reluctant but said I'd play sweeper if the opposition were from near the bottom of the league, which Dessie told me was the case.

On the day of the game I was speaking to Dessie when I saw that the other team were all young lads aged between 19 and 25, wearing matching tracksuits and looking very business-like.

Dessie claimed they were a "shit team" but that's not how they looked to me. As they walked past, I saw 'Brigg Town FC' written on the back of their tracksuits. Brigg were at the top of the league.

Having not trained for three years, I had a little pot belly and there were shouts from the crowd of "has he got the ball down his shirt?" I was not looking forward to chasing after these young lads. Anyway, we only went and beat them 2-1 and I lasted the whole game. After the match, Dessie tried to get me to play every week. There was not a chance of that happening.

## MASTERS FOOTBALL

I did take part in a few of the veterans' tournaments for Everton and Leeds a few years ago. You have to nominate your preferred team and mine was Everton. At that stage Everton had a full squad so I ended up playing for Leeds. Later on, Everton were short of numbers so I transferred to them.

The Masters should be for the likes of Jan Molby and me, who are into their mid-to-late 40s and are not fit. When you watch it now, some of them are still playing league football. I don't think the paying audience want to see lads who are still playing. It should be about blokes with a pot belly and no hair. I think the enjoyment has gone out of it and that's why a lot of lads don't play in it anymore.

## MANAGERIAL INFLUENCES

When I managed Donny, I tried to be my own person. I could be nasty but I could be their best mate as well. Watching the World Cup, that seemed to be the approach of Diego Maradona with Argentina. Fabio Capello took the opposite view. I think you need a distance from the players while also being friendly and approachable. You understood Billy Bremner was the boss but you knew if you did the business, he'd have his arm around you. I didn't consciously try to follow the styles of any of my managers but I'm sure they all influenced me.

I found it incredible that Glynn and I were finished up after less than two years. Sir Alex Ferguson or Capello couldn't have done a better job of raising Donny from the depths. We left them with a professional set-up: the crowds were up and the training facilities were superb. I'll probably never manage again but I know I've got something to offer.

## MY OTHER HALF, JOANNE

Being married to a footballer must be difficult, especially when we were going away or on a night out. You needed to go out and unwind because there was a lot of pressure. At Doncaster you wanted to win and get the bonus money because you weren't on massive money. At Leeds there was the pressure of trying to get them back into the top league. At Everton they were used to winning things and you were under pressure to keep your place. As a footballer, you could just coast along and be happy picking up a certain wage, but the top players always strive for more.

Joanne was great throughout my career, looking after the kids. She's been a superb mother and great wife. There have been disagreements along the way, but I can't speak highly enough of her.

## BROTHER GLYNN

Glynn is my brother and a friend. We left Doncaster at the same time in 1985, with me going to Leeds while he signed for Sheffield Wednesday. Sadly he was wasted at Hillsborough because of their long-ball approach. I'm not knocking their then manager, Howard Wilkinson, because he had a lot of success, but the style of play didn't suit my brother. I remember watching one of his first games for Wednesday and he was superb. However, he told me he'd received a bollocking in the dressing room for not being more direct in his passing.

He was technically better than me but I probably had more desire, greater aggression and more pace. If our kid played for Everton when I did, he'd have been outstanding.

He's worked extremely hard to get where he is today. He was

a coach at West Ham and Charlton, and now he's assistant manager at Leeds and for Northern Ireland. He is one of the best coaches in the country. The former Aston Villa manager John Gregory told me how impressive he found Glynn when they did coaching courses together. He has an excellent reputation in the game.

## OVER-COMPLICATION

To me, a game of football is a game of football, whether you are playing for England or in Sunday league. I never had a psychologist telling me to focus. I didn't need that. I'm sure Peter Reid and Graeme Sharp didn't need that. There are a lot of people involved in football today who have no need to be there. It's got very technical with Prozone and sensors monitoring how far you run during a game. I didn't need to know how many miles I'd run, I knew if I'd played well or not.

Yes, you've got to eat properly and drink the right things but you don't need a psychologist telling you how to win a game of football. The benches are full, with an entourage of 13 or 14 people. Why do they all do?

## COACHING BADGES

In March 2003 Peter Reid was given the manager's job at Leeds United after Terry Venables left. He asked me to join his backroom team but as I'd never taken a coaching qualification, I wasn't able to accept his invitation. I was advised that even if I was fast-tracked, it would be a year before I got the necessary qualifications. That was the end of it.

I'm very anti-coaching badges. With all the experience I have in the game, I don't see why I should be forced into going on a coaching course. If you've had a football education all your life, then why do you need a badge?

I have stood on the line and watched my kids play football, getting no guidance from the coaches. These people are supposed to be more qualified than I am. Deep down, they don't have a clue what they are talking about. Other parents have approached me and asked: "Ian, can't you get involved?" I can't because I don't have any badges.

As a father of kids who play the sport, I'm sure they'd rather be taught by a professional footballer than someone who has never kicked a ball in a competitive game. To make our kids better players the FA should allow ex-professionals without badges to coach. I'm sure there are loads of ex-pros who would love to get involved.

England aren't going to win the World Cup in the next 20 years, given the way the sport is run. The England Under-19 team who took part in the recent European Championship were well below the standard of Spain and France. More ex-pros need to be involved from under-10s right through to full-time academy level. The FA needs to open their eyes.

People have said to me that I could earn great money in Dubai or America if I get these qualifications but I refuse to do them. In contrast, Glynn has every coaching badge under the sun. He has a different attitude to me where coaching is concerned.

The clincher for me was when Eddie Gray was asked to take over from Peter Reid at Leeds in November 2003. He had been at the top level since he was 14 years old but they couldn't make him a permanent appointment because he didn't have a badge. He had been a player, manager in the 1980s and then youth-team coach. Why? Why do you need a badge? It's completely ridiculous.

## THE MODERN FOOTBALLER

It's less fun to be a footballer now. They are rewarded on a far greater scale than I experienced and good luck to them. You still have to earn the respect of the fans though.

There is now a big distance between players and supporters. We would be in the pub, mingling and drinking with them. Modern players can't do that. They are treated like superstars and fans can't get near them. If they get a picture or an autograph with a certain player, they think they've won the pools. The footballers' existence is so far removed from the normal supporter who earns £300 a week and works in a factory. Some players think they are special. They're not – they're just lads who have a gift for playing football.

Not all get above themselves. I recently spent time with Everton's midfielder Jack Rodwell and his dad at a golf day. You couldn't meet a nicer kid. He sat and listened to Graham Stuart, Alan Harper and myself reminiscing about old stories. He was loving it and showed an interest in my children. Jack has been brought up the right way. He has enormous talent and can go on to play for England and earn vast amounts of money. Hopefully the kid won't change. The day you start thinking you are something special you alienate the fans.

## RICH CLUBS' DOMINATION – AND CHANGES I'D LIKE TO SEE

The money that has flowed into football over the last 20 years is phenomenal. Manchester United, Arsenal, Chelsea and Liverpool have moved further away from the other clubs because of the vast sums they've earned in European football. Manchester City are about to join them and Tottenham are close. Those clubs are going to remain where they are for years to come.

I would like to see fewer foreign players competing in our league. A maximum of four in the squad is enough. The best of the overseas talent surrounded by British players is the ideal scenario. I don't think it will ever come to pass but if England want to have a better chance at international level, you have to have English players involved in big matches. There are too many average foreign players in the English game. I've loved watching the best from abroad, the likes of Cristiano Ronaldo, Fernando Torres and Mikel Arteta, but it's wrong when you see average players on big money who are keeping out British kids. Look at Liverpool; their squad has been filled with foreigners from the youth squad to first-team level. How many of the young foreign players they've brought in over the last five years have progressed to the first team and proved a success? Not one.

## YOUTH FOOTBALL

Having watched my sons play from six years old, I've seen that the facilities for kids' football in this country are horrendous. Pitches are a joke, the players have to change at home before they even get to the match and often there are no nets. It's not like that in Germany and Holland. The FA should be putting their money into grass-roots football. Young children shouldn't have to dodge dog muck or broken glass.

I am totally against kids being taken on by club academies at seven years old. Play with your mates, your school team, your Sunday league team and enjoy it. There is too much pressure at a young age. Nine year olds are left in tears if clubs let them go. They should not be taking them on until they are 12 or 13.

My son Jordan turned 16 in 2010 and joined Leeds United, but I pulled him out of Doncaster Rovers when he was 12 because the other lads were outgrowing him and the game was passing him by. He needed a couple of years to mature as a lad and grow up a little. Being rejected by clubs at a young age can destroy a lad's confidence. Jordan has matured in the body now and by 20 he could be a player. Will he get that opportunity? Clubs are after a quick fix; they want the finished article at 18. That's not always feasible. People mature at different stages.

## BOSMAN RULING

Allowing players to move for free at the end of their contract was a major change in the game. I wish it had been an option when I played. Clubs are forced into awarding players long contracts because they don't want to lose them for free two or three years down the line. It makes some of them a little bit complacent. The ruling isn't fair to clubs but it's great for players.

When I left Leeds, I had another year and a bit remaining on my contract. If the Bosman ruling had been in effect, I could have seen that out and received higher wages out of the cash the buying club saved on the transfer fee. Alternatively, I could have asked Leeds to give me £100,000 out of the fee Everton were prepared to pay.

However, if I'd chosen to see out my contract, I could have picked up a serious injury or my form could have dipped. If that had been the case, Everton and Liverpool may no longer have been interested in me.

Because of how easy it is to pick up players on free transfers, Bosman has brought a lot of average foreigners to English football. That's not a good thing.

## VIDEO TECHNOLOGY

I'm all for using technology for goal-line decisions. There's a move to have two extra assistants but I don't think that's necessary. I love the talking points that football provides, such as penalty decisions. Five officials on the pitch is ludicrous. Three is sufficient but we need goal-line technology – Frank Lampard's 'goal' against Germany during the World Cup demonstrated that.

## REFEREES

Amongst the current officials, I really like Howard Webb. I watched Jordan's Doncaster schools' Under-16s cup final and Howard, who is from Rotherham, was the referee. He was superb with the kids, talking to them but staying out of the way and letting them get on with the game. He told me he likes to referee a youth cup final in Doncaster every year. This was a couple of months before the World Cup. The kids absolutely loved him and he happily posed for photographs.

I felt sorry for Howard during the World Cup final. He could have turned it into a farce within half-an-hour by showing red cards to two or three Holland players. If he'd done that, people would have said he spoiled the game. When you watch him in the Premier League, you can tell that the players respect him. He's one of the very best referees.

They receive plenty of criticism but referees don't have it easy these days. All I want to see from a game of football is two teams giving their all with some good tackling. It frustrates me when I see players diving and constantly whingeing.

In my time, Keith Hackett and Keith Cooper were brilliant,

whilst you couldn't have any banter with Clive Thomas or George Tyson. The best referees don't interfere or don't want to be noticed. If I moaned at Hackett and told him he was having a nightmare, he'd say: "You're not playing too well yourself." You could relate to referees like him. You want a bit of respect and banter.

## DONCASTER ROVERS – 2010

They aren't going to go any higher than the Championship. There are clubs in that division who attract bigger crowds and are better placed financially. If Donny can maintain their status for as long as they can, it will be a massive achievement. It's only 12 years since they were virtually extinct and last season they were playing Newcastle United. Nobody could have believed that when they were going to Forest Green, Dover, Hednesford and Leigh RMI.

The fans are happy with the way they play. They know that they're not going to win the league but if they have a decent season, that's good enough.

## LEEDS UNITED – 2010

I was in a catch-22 position when Doncaster played Leeds in the League One play-off final in 2008. I did slightly favour Donny, but I didn't want either side to lose.

Being promoted to the Championship in 2009/10 was great but there is still a lot of rebuilding to do. Money needs to be spent.

The fans are second-to-none; they'll follow them home and away. I want to see the big clubs with large fan-bases and good stadiums in the Premier League. That's where Leeds belong.

Glynn told me they took 4-5,000 to Bristol Rovers on a Tuesday night in October 2009. They deserve to be in the Premier League and hopefully they'll be back in the top division soon.

## EVERTON – 2010

I experienced massive ups when I first arrived at Everton, and then witnessed a gradual decline. They've struggled since the heyday of the 1980s. For Everton not to be challenging for trophies is a joke. In the 1990s we were mostly remembered for games where we achieved results to keep us in the Premier League. There was a high with the FA Cup win in 1995 but they didn't build on that.

From that period until David Moyes's arrival, they brought players in who weren't good enough. You could understand why the fans were getting frustrated. Moyes has been a breath of fresh air. He's a good person, has done a terrific job and he works his socks off. Okay, he's not won a trophy yet but he's built a squad capable of challenging and beating top teams.

The stadium is a very big issue. I would love to see a new ground and the club need it but, as a Yorkshireman, who am I to comment on a sensitive issue like that?

In other areas the club has moved forward. Bellefield was unique, the best of its kind in the 1960s, but the new Finch Farm training complex is incredible. The lads have the best of everything.

Everton Football Club is on a high, with a great manager, players and training facility. All we need now are some trophies, even if it might be a few years before the top clubs can be challenged. It's going to be difficult but Moyes is the man, definitely. How much longer he will stay, I don't know. He's been there for over eight years and you can become stale. Saying that, he is loved by most Evertonians and he loves the club.

## A LIFE IN FOOTBALL

All I wanted to do was make a living out of playing football. End of. I was playing with my mates in a little mining village when I was 14. To go from that to playing for Everton in a Merseyside derby took a lot of doing. The injury stopped me from having an even better career. Maybe if I'd looked after myself a little bit better when I was injured, I might have returned faster and played for longer.

I'm glad I played when I did, although you'd love the money they earn now. The Everton team of 1987 could handle themselves in any era. They were great players and would be earning £100,000 a week now. I was on £500 a week when I signed for Leeds, £1,000 when I moved to Everton and £2,000 when I signed an improved contract. We were paid well for our time and had a lot of fun on and off the field. There were some great highs, I met some great people and there were plenty of laughs along the way.

# CHAPTER 13

## Ian's 'Player Profile', with a 21st century slant

**Favourite food?**

*"Steak, fish and chips"*

**Favourite TV programme?**

*"Fawlty Towers, Benny Hill"*

**Favourite musician/bands?**

*"George Benson, The Jam"*

**Professional ambition?**

*"To play in the First Division"*

**Ian Snodin, Doncaster programme 'Player Profiles',
1981-83**

## HEIGHT

I'm just short of 5ft 11ins now. I was probably only about 5ft 7ins when I first got in the Donny team. I didn't feel at a disadvantage because I wasn't playing centre-forward or centre-half.

## WEIGHT

This was my main issue at a younger age because I could easily get pushed off the ball but I had always been fiery, even from five or six years old. I could tackle and look after myself. In my early days Alan Little, the brother of former Aston Villa manager Brian, was brought in from Barnsley and acted as my minder. He took me under his wing and even taught me to drive on Donny's massive car park.

Weight is a problem for me now in a different way. It's 14-and-a-half stone. I'd like to be a stone-and-a-half lighter.

## HOME

I live in a village called Trumfleet in Doncaster. There are only six houses and we are three miles from the nearest shop. However, it's only 20 minutes from the town centre and 10 minutes from school for the children. We're surrounded by farmers' fields, the girls have got horses, and there are sheep and cows. It's perfect for me, although the kids get a little fed up now and again being away from their mates.

## CHILDREN

We have five children. Zoe, 24, is the eldest. Ian is 22, Jordan is 16, Reece is 13 and Brooke is 11. I also have a granddaughter, Maddison, who is two.

## CARS

My first car was a Volkswagen Golf. It cost me £750 and was a horrendous green colour. I had a lovely sponsored Saab at Leeds and we were given a £10,000 allowance to put towards a vehicle when I joined Everton. At the moment I've got a 4x4 Kia and I'm due to get a Mercedes soon. I've never been particularly bothered by cars; as long as it gets you from A to B and it looks alright, that's all that matters.

## NICKNAME
Snods. When I came to Everton it became Snowy, which seems to be my Liverpool nickname.

## FAVOURITE BRITISH PLAYER, PAST AND PRESENT
When I supported Chelsea, I was a massive fan of Ray Wilkins. When I was at Doncaster and Leeds, I really admired Bryan Robson. I thought our respective games were similar in my early years – I could go from box-to-box and tackle, although he scored more than me. I played against him a couple of times and when I was in the England squad, he was the captain. What a player.

I look at it from a totally different perspective now. I admire Wayne Rooney and the way he wants to play. To some it's a job – he would happily join in a kickabout in the street. He earns a lot of money but he'd play for nothing. Being an Evertonian, I also admire the players who want to play for the club. For someone like Alan Stubbs, Everton was his life.

## FAVOURITE TEAM
Everton, no question about it. If Everton and Donny were playing each other, I'd want Everton to win. If I was to put it into order it would be Everton first, Doncaster second and Leeds third. Donny gave me my grounding, I thought Leeds was a massive club and I had the best eight years of my life at Everton, even with the time I missed through injury.

## FAVOURITE STADIUM
I would say the Bernabeu in Madrid. We lost heavily in a friendly but it was a great place to play. I loved running out at Goodison and I also liked playing at Anfield, especially when it wasn't segregated. The atmosphere on derby day in my early years at Everton was unbelievable.

## BEST GOAL SCORED

An overhead kick playing for Leeds in a pre-season friendly at Exeter. It came from a corner and I volleyed it in from the penalty spot into the top corner. The one that sticks in my mind for its meaning is my first league goal for Doncaster against Aldershot.

## MOST DIFFICULT OPPONENT

In midfield, Bryan Robson. As a full-back, John Barnes. He was outstanding and a couple of times I thought he was unplayable. I get on great with him now and he always says I was one of his toughest opponents because I liked to kick him early doors. I caught him with a few beauties.

## MAGIC MOMENT

I've got a few. Making my full debut for Donny and my first game for England youth against Scotland in February 1982 are two of them. It was a very proud moment when I stood in line and heard the national anthem, looking down at the three lions on my shirt. No matter what sport and what level, to represent your country is the pinnacle. I'm very patriotic and that was a fantastic feeling.

## BIGGEST DISAPPOINTMENT

My injury. At the time it happened (early 1989) there were four or five right-backs in contention to play for England: Gary Stevens, Mel Sterland, Paul Parker, myself and Lee Dixon, who was just emerging for Arsenal. I was quick, I could defend, I could get forward, I was composed on the ball and I could deliver good crosses into the box. I was on the verge of making my England debut and my hamstring went. I didn't realise then that I wouldn't be over it for three-and-a-half years.

## FAVOURITE OTHER SPORTS

I like all sports. Whatever sport is on television, I will watch it. My favourites outside football are cricket, golf and badminton. I love all aspects of cricket and will happily watch a five-day Test match or a Twenty20 game. Playing golf is always enjoyable, although my two sons beat me these days. I was half decent at badminton but I don't play so much now. I also like watching horse racing.

## FAVOURITE TV PROGRAMMES

I used to love watching comedies like *Fawlty Towers* and *Bread* when I was younger. Now I enjoy watching cookery programmes like *Masterchef*. I'm not a great cook but I'll have a go.

## MISCELLANEOUS LIKES AND DISLIKES

I like people to be polite. There is no effort in saying please or thank you. I don't like ignorant people.

## FAVOURITE MUSICIAN/SINGER

When I've had a drink, I like a sing-song on the karaoke – George Benson has always been a favourite – but I've never been a big buyer of CDs or albums. I've only been to a few concerts; Wet Wet Wet with the Missus so she could see Marti Pellow, and Michael Jackson at Aintree Racecourse in 1988. Graeme Sharp arranged some cheap tickets for a few of us but when it came to the night we were across the Melling Road, miles away from the stage. You needed binoculars to see the big screen, never mind Jacko himself. After a few songs we got off and headed to the pub.

## FAVOURITE FOOD

I love a fillet steak, a Sunday roast with Yorkshire puddings and fish and chips out of the wrapping while on the coast – somewhere like Bridlington, Cleethorpes or Scarborough. It's traditional foods for me. When I first came to Everton I'd never had a foreign meal but over the last 20 years I've grown to enjoy Chinese, Indian or Thai dishes. Initially the lads could not believe it when we'd visit a Chinese restaurant because Neville Southall and I would order chicken and chips. Sharpy tried to get me to eat smoked fish one. I never entertained the idea. It was either prawn cocktail and steak or a roast dinner for me.

## FAVOURITE DRINK

When I was younger I had to have lime with my lager. I love a vodka and coke – Neil Pointon and I would often drink Black Russians when we were at Everton. I've grown to enjoy Guinness but I need a touch of blackcurrant with it. I enjoy most drinks but I can categorically say I've never taken a single drug in my life – I can't understand why people do.

## FAVOURITE COUNTRY VISITED

I love America. As a footballer you visit many places but you don't get to see a lot outside the hotel, the training facilities and stadiums. I find beach and pool holidays boring so I like fly-drive breaks in the States, which I think are good for parents and children. I visited Mauritius with Everton and that was magnificent.

## FAVOURITE ACTOR/ACTRESS

It used to be Charles Bronson. Now I really like Jim Carrey for his facial expressions and the effort he puts in to his performances.

## CLOSEST FRIENDS

There's Alick Jeffrey, who I mentioned earlier in the book and who still works for Doncaster. Kev Harle, the brother of my former team-mate Dave, is another, and a lad called Dave Rice who is a good pal. I would like to think I've got 20 to 30 mates who I could rely on or phone up to arrange a social evening.

## CLOSEST FRIEND IN FOOTBALL

I was close to Ian Baird when I was at Leeds, and Neil Pointon, Kevin Sheedy, Graeme Sharp and Peter Beardsley at Everton. Again, I'd like to think I got on with most people at every club I played for.

## BIGGEST INFLUENCE ON YOUR CAREER
My dad and Billy Bremner.

## CAREER AMBITIONS
I'm in the process of setting up a sports management company. The way Billy Bremner looked after me, I would like to offer that same service to 10 or 15 lads on our books. There are many good players who go off the rails. You need help and guidance when you're younger and I want to offer advice to young kids just coming into the game, and their parents. I enjoy my radio and corporate work and would love to keep doing that.

## CHILDHOOD HERO
Geoff Boycott. I used to imagine I was him when I played cricket with my pals.

## BEST PLAYER I'VE PLAYED AGAINST IN MY POSITION
In midfield, Lothar Matthaus. In 1987 we played Bayern Munich at Goodison as part of the Football League's Centenary celebrations. I was up against Matthaus in midfield and he had everything. At right-back, probably Gary Stevens.

## LIVELIEST CHARACTER YOU'VE COME ACROSS IN FOOTBALL
Adrian Heath was the life and soul of any gathering.

## WORST MOMENT ON A FOOTBALL PITCH
A big disappointment was when I was sent off against Charlton at Goodison in March 1987. I went up for header with Andy Peake and as the ball came towards us, he tried to elbow me in the face. I stepped back and kicked him up the arse. There was a confrontation between Peake and myself and the other players surrounded us. Kevin Ratcliffe grabbed me and put my arms around my back. While I was restrained, Peake caught me with two punches. There was blood on my face and the referee sent off the two of us. I was fuming – I'd not really done anything, been caught with two beauties and was gone.

I saw Peake disappearing towards the tunnel and decided I'd have him. Our reserve goalkeeper Bobby Mimms tried to stop me as I yelled: "I'm going to kill him." Someone from the Charlton coaching staff saw me and pushed Peake into the away dressing room before quickly locking the door. I banged on the door and demanded he come out – but he never did. I saw him at the PFA awards the following year when I'd had a drink. He apologised and we had a laugh about the incident.

There were one or two other occasions when I saw red. I was sent off at Hereford when I was Doncaster player-manager. I played for the first 60 minutes, came off and stood by the bench with my kit on. I had a pop at the referee and the fourth official, who had told me to sit down. He called the referee over and I was ordered away from the bench. I ended up sat alongside the Donny chairman wearing my kit, shinpads and boots.

Then there was one at West Brom for Leeds. I went into a tackle with Barry Cowdrill and while we were lying on the floor, he kicked out at me. I got up and stood over him, with my boot over his face, threatening to trample on him. I had no intention of doing so but Carlton Palmer raced over and rugby-tackled me to the floor. As punches were being thrown, the referee jumped in and sent us both off. I sat in the dressing room gutted at what had happened. After a few minutes I heard footsteps, the door opened and John Stiles walked in. He'd been brought on as a sub and subsequently sent off.

## FAVOURITE PLACE VISITED ON A FOOTBALL TRIP

Dublin and Drogheda in Ireland. We played Drogheda and their chairman got on our bus before the game and announced: "Let's get this game out of the way – there's some serious drinking to be done." Sir Philip Carter, the Everton chairman and Colin Harvey, the manager, were sat at the front and they both baulked. We won the game and I was named Man of the Match, for which I received a lovely crystal trophy. More importantly, I was presented with about 200 vouchers for free drinks in all the local pubs. The other lads got about 20 or 30. I was popular on that trip. The Irish are really warm people.

## TV SHOW ON WHICH I'D MOST LIKE TO APPEAR

I'd like to go on *The Weakest Link* and go up against Anne Robinson. She's very good and I like her barbed comments to contestants. I'd have to appear on an ex-footballers edition because some of the questions are very difficult. If I was to go on, I think it would be quite confrontational.

## FAVOURITE SPORTS COMMENTATOR

I love David Lloyd on cricket; he is exceptional. Not only is he knowledgeable about cricket, his comments are superb when the cameras pan into the crowd. Geoff Boycott is fantastic. Certain people have the right voice for particular sports. Alan Green divides opinion but his voice is great for listening to a football match on the radio. David Coleman was perfect for athletics, Peter Alliss likewise on golf.

## FAVOURITE ITEM OF CLOTHING

I've never been into fashion in any way. At the moment it's a pair of jeans that I've nicked off my son. I wasn't brought up to be interested in designer gear – there's no airs and graces or frills about me.

## BEST AND WORST DRESSED TEAM-MATES

Pat Nevin and Neil Pointon were the worst, definitely. Pat had a long coat that he bought from Oxfam for £3.50, which he wore over a suit. Pat was actually the first person I ever knew who owned a Filofax. Whenever we went on a trip, he'd note down the museums and places of interest he wanted to visit. He would go off and sightsee while the rest of us would automatically head for the first bar. The lads would rip him but he would always rejoin us and have a glass of red white. He was different to a typical footballer of the time – most of us weren't as intelligent as him and just wanted to drink.

As for Pointon, he thought he looked smart but white socks

with shoes wasn't a good look. Graeme Sharp spent quite a lot on clothes and looked the part most of the time.

Going back to Pat Nevin, in a Sunday Times feature in 2007 he named me in the best XI he'd played with or against. Diego Maradona was one of my team-mates! Pat is a regular at Goodison Park and when I saw him after that article was published, I went straight up to him and thanked him.

## SUPERSTITIONS

I never really had any but later in my career if we'd won a game, I would wear the same underpants and socks for the next match, although they would be washed in the meantime!

I don't recall many of my team-mates having any major superstitions but Colin Douglas, a Scot who I played with at Doncaster, liked to have a shot of whisky immediately before home matches.

## FAVOURITE AWAY GROUND TO WATCH FOOTBALL FROM

Pride Park and Stamford Bridge – the feed in the press room at both grounds was magnificent.

## WORST GAME EVER SEEN

I covered a match at Chester for Sky where, for 44 minutes, there wasn't a shot or tackle of any relevance. Rob McCaffrey and myself didn't have a clue what we were going to talk about at half-time. Thankfully, there was a player sent off and a penalty in the 45th minute that saved us.

## THE MOUSTACHE

I had no need to shave until I was 19 and the moustache remained untouched until I was 24. Even then, nobody in my family realised I had shaved it until I remarked: "Notice anything different?" In the 1980s loads of players had a moustache. Brian Kilcline, the former captain of Coventry City, had the most impressive facial hair of any footballer I came across.

## FAVOURITE SWEETS

I love my sweets. When I was a boy, my mum used to send me to a general store in the village, Hodgkinson and Son, to pick up bread and potatoes. The potatoes were kept in the back of the shop so when the owner disappeared, I would fill my pockets with sweets from the counter in front of me. I was always happy to go and regularly asked: "Mum, do you need any more potatoes?" It was so wrong but all of us did it.

## PRE-MATCH MEALS

When I first got into the Donny team, it was steak (well done) and chips. After a while the chips disappeared and a few mushrooms found their way on to my plate. Later on it tended to be chicken and beans.

When I was at Everton, a few of us preferred to get up early and have a full English breakfast between 8-9am. Kev Ratcliffe was fond of that. After the breakfast, I wouldn't have a thing to eat until after the game. There would be a cup of tea at 12pm and that was it. The likes of Graeme Sharp would have a lie-in and come down at 11.30 for beans on toast or chicken.

## FAVOURITE FILMS

I wouldn't say it was a favourite but I watched Alfred Hitchcock's *The Birds* when I was about nine. For months afterwards I was terrified if I saw a flock of crows or starlings. It took me two years to get over it.

## FAVOURITE SONGS

### Cool Water: Frankie Laine

My dad played it all the time and I learnt all the words.

### Big Bad John: Jimmy Dean

It's about a miner. I played it to my kids a couple of years ago and my youngest daughter, who was seven at the time, liked it, learnt the words and sang it to my dad.

### Give Me The Night: George Benson

When I joined Leeds, I sang it on a squad night out and John Sheridan was very impressed. He still calls me George now.

### Rapper's Delight: The Sugarhill Gang

It's a long song but I know all the words.

### Mustang Sally: Wilson Pickett/The Commitments

As long as it is sung by Neil Ruddock and myself in Southport.

### Love Is All Around: Wet Wet Wet

I went to Tenerife with my eldest son, Ian, about five years ago. Alick Jeffrey was with us and one night we were in a bar with karaoke going on. Alick encouraged me to get up. I looked through the songbook but nothing grabbed me. Eventually I chose 'Love Is All Around' by Wet Wet Wet. Ian begged me not to embarrass him but I wasn't going to be talked out of it. When I was singing, Ian's mouth fell open as he realised I was actually quite good.

### Do They Know It's Christmas: Band Aid

I love Christmas, especially now that I don't have to leave the family and play football, and I love this song.

## WHAT MAKES ME LAUGH

I enjoy life and I get the most out of it. I like funny, genuine people.

## RULE CHANGES I'D LIKE TO SEE IN FOOTBALL

I don't like players having to go off the pitch and come back on after receiving treatment on an injury. I'd also like the offside rule to be clearer by getting rid of all this phase one and phase two nonsense. I don't understand it and I've been in football all my life. I don't think anybody understands it. There's not a lot that I'd change, other than a foreign player restriction.

## MOST SUCCESSFUL BET

I had a place pot accumulator at Cheltenham that came in. I put £26 on it and won £3,500. I've never been one to bet thousands, usually £20, £40 or £100 maximum. I'd certainly have been wealthier if I hadn't been a betting man, but I enjoy it. Anyone who does it gets a buzz out of winning.

## JOBS BEFORE FOOTBALL

The only proper job I ever had was when I went on a family holiday to Rhyl for two weeks. I was 14 or 15 and didn't want to hang about with my mum and dad or sit on the beach at that age. After two days I saw a part-time job advertised at an amusement arcade. I decided I wanted to work there. The role was to sit in a booth and fill the change machine. I went to see the owner, who took me on. I was paid £10 per day and stayed there for the rest of the holiday, going home with £70. My parents came in on a couple of occasions and asked for five 10p pieces.

## FAVOURITE SPORTS PERSONALITY

I loved Michael Jordan, the basketball player. I thought he was an incredible sportsman and my son Jordan is named after him. I bought a couple of videos about him, which showed his training routines and most memorable moments on court. I showed them to the Doncaster lads and they were as much in awe of him as I was.

## BEST AND WORST KITS WORN

My favourite one was the Leeds United kit, the all-white. I loved it. There was something about that look – it just felt right. The worst one was the salmon pink away strip Everton brought out in 1992 – that was awful. I did score a goal in that kit, though – in 1993 at Selhurst Park against Wimbledon in front of 3,039, which remains the lowest post-war attendance in the top division. I went running off to celebrate and there wasn't anybody there, just a ball boy.

## FIRST XI FROM THE PLAYERS I'VE PLAYED ALONGSIDE

Neville Southall

Gary Stevens    Dave Watson    Kevin Ratcliffe    Glynn Snodin

Trevor Steven    Peter Reid    John Sheridan    Kevin Sheedy

Graeme Sharp    Peter Beardsley

Substitute: Adrian Heath

# STATS

A career in figures – Ian's near 20-year playing record from his first-team debut for Doncaster Rovers, age 16, playing against Bournemouth in the Fourth Division in the 1979/80 season – through to his player/manager spell back at the club where it all began at the end of the 20th century

## IAN SNODIN

## PLAYING RECORD, CLUB CAREER

### DONCASTER ROVERS
### THIRD/FOURTH DIVISION
### 1979-1985

|  | Apps | Goals |
|---|---|---|
| League | 188 | 24 |
| FA Cup | 12 | 1 |
| League Cup | 9 | 1 |
| Others | 5 | 0 |
| *TOTAL* | *214* | *26* |

### LEEDS UNITED
### SECOND DIVISION
### 1985-1987

|  | Apps | Goals |
|---|---|---|
| League | 51 | 6 |
| FA Cup | 1 | 0 |
| League Cup | 3 | 2 |
| *TOTAL* | *55* | *8* |

### EVERTON
### FIRST DIVISION/PREMIER LEAGUE
### 1987-1995

Everton

|  | Apps | Goals |
|---|---|---|
| League | 148 | 3 |
| FA Cup | 26 | 2 |
| League Cup | 23 | 2 |
| Others | 4 | 0 |
| *TOTAL* | *201* | *7* |

**IAN SNODIN**

## PLAYING RECORD, CLUB CAREER

**SUNDERLAND**
FIRST DIVISION
1994

|  | Apps | Goals |
|---|---|---|
| League | 6 | 0 |
| *TOTAL* | *6* | *0* |

**OLDHAM ATHLETIC**
FIRST DIVISION
1995-1997

|  | Apps | Goals |
|---|---|---|
| League | 57 | 0 |
| FA Cup | 1 | 0 |
| League Cup | 0 | 0 |
| Others | 1 | 0 |
| *TOTAL* | *59* | *0* |

**SCARBOROUGH**
THIRD DIVISION
1997-1998

|  | Apps | Goals |
|---|---|---|
| League | 35 | 0 |
| FA Cup | 1 | 0 |
| League Cup | 1 | 0 |
| Others | 1 | 0 |
| *TOTAL* | *38* | *0* |

## IAN SNODIN

### PLAYING RECORD, CLUB CAREER

**DONCASTER ROVERS**
CONFERENCE
1998-2000

|  | Apps | Goals |
|---|---|---|
| Conference | 13 | 0 |
| FA Cup | 2 | 0 |
| *TOTAL* | *15* | *0* |

## IAN SNODIN

### PLAYING RECORD, CLUB CAREER TOTAL

|  | Apps | Goals |
|---|---|---|
| League/Conference | 498 | 33 |
| FA Cup | 43 | 3 |
| League Cup | 36 | 5 |
| Others | 11 | 0 |
| *TOTAL* | *588* | *41* |

## IAN SNODIN

### PLAYING RECORD, CLUB CAREER DISMISSALS

| For | Against | Venue | Comp | Date |
| --- | --- | --- | --- | --- |
| Doncaster | Swindon | Away | League | 03/12/1983 |
| Leeds | Blackburn | Away | League | 23/08/1986 |
| Leeds | West Brom | Away | League | 06/12/1986 |
| Everton | Charlton | Home | League | 21/03/1987 |
| Oldham | Sunderland | Home | League | 14/01/1995 |
| Scarborough | Scunthorpe | Home | Lge Cup | 12/08/1997 |
| Scarborough | Chester | Away | League | 02/05/1998 |

## IAN SNODIN

## PLAYING RECORD, INTERNATIONAL CAREER

 ### ENGLAND YOUTH
### 1982

|  | Apps | Goals |
|---|---|---|
| 23/02/1982 v Scotland (0-1) | 1 | 0 |
| *TOTAL* | *1* | *0* |

 ### ENGLAND UNDER-21S
### 1984-1985

|  | Apps | Goals |
|---|---|---|
| 13/11/1984 v Turkey (0-0) | 1 | 0 |
| 27/02/1985 v Israel (2-1) | 1 | 0 |
| 30/04/1985 v Romania (0-0) | 1 | 0 |
| 21/05/1985 v Finland (1-3) | 1 | 0 |
| *TOTAL* | *4* | *0* |

 ### ENGLAND B
### 1987-1990

|  | Apps | Goals |
|---|---|---|
| 14/10/1987 v Malta (2-0) | 1 | 0 |
| 27/03/1990 v R. Ireland (1-4) | 1 | 0 |
| *TOTAL* | *2* | *0* |

# INDEX

# OTHER SPORT MEDIA PUBLICATIONS

Updated third edition
of the popular
release, celebrating
Everton games and
bizarre moments

The fascinating story
of David France's
heralded collection
of EFC memorabilia

An amusing look at
the best of the worst
clothing crimes from
some of the biggest
names in football

Fascinating account
of the legendary
football genius
between 1971-1973

A unique look at
Everton's kits from
their formation in
1878 to the present

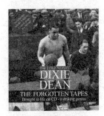

Historic CD book
from interviews
given by Everton's
greatest-ever player

**All of these titles, and more, are available to order by calling
0845 143 0001 or you can buy online at www.merseyshop.com**

# SNOD THIS
# THIS
## for a
# LAUGH